Social and Political Inquiry

A Working Introduction to the
Social Sciences

John D. May
Karl J. Bemesderfer

Duxbury Press

A Division of Wadsworth Publishing Company, Inc.

© 1972 by Wadsworth Publishing Company, Inc., Belmont, California 94002. All rights reserved. No part of this book may be reproduced, stored in a retrieval system, or transcribed, in any form or by any means, electronic, mechanical, photocopying, recording, or otherwise, without the prior written permission of the publisher, Duxbury Press, a division of Wadsworth Publishing Company, Inc., Belmont, California.

L.C. Cat. Card No. 72-075106
ISBN 0-87872-026-X
Printed in the United States of America

1 2 3 4 5 6 7 8 9 10—76 75 74 73 72

Contents

*Exercise
number*

	Preface	v
	Introduction	vii

Section One.   Reading Auguries

Objective Conditions

1	Location of a Safe Haven	3
2	Effectiveness in Law Enforcement	4
3	Electoral Participation	4
4	Medical Progress	4
5	The Spread of Knowledge	5
6	Defense Capabilities	5
7	Cheating on Examinations	5
8	Guaging Quality Control	6

Subjective Conditions

9	Student Opinion on Homework Loads	7
10	Community Opinion on Tax Reform	7
11	Community Opinion on Busing	8
12	Community Opinion on "Escalation"	8
13	Change in Community Opinion on "Escalation"	8
14	Testing for Poll Reliability: Prediction Versus Actuality	9
15	Quality of Responses	10

Exercise
number

Section Two. Sorting Out Cause and Effect

Juvenile Delinquency

16	Race?	14
17	Bad Company?	14
18	Bad and Older Company?	15
19	Family Size and Birth Order?	15

"Athleticism" and Neurosis

20	What TIME Said Doctor Little Said	16
21	What Doctor Little Said	17

Student Radicalism

22	Sanity, Intellect, and Political Orientation	27

Political Forms: Democracy

23	Is Oligarchy Unavoidable?	43
24	Does Democracy Require Affluence?	46

Social Forms: Equality

25	Is Equality Attainable?	65

Section Three. Appraising Policies

26	Equity and Wage-Price Guideposts	79
27	Should Conventional A–B–C–D–F Grading Be Abandoned?	79
28	Equity in Rent Control	83
29	Liberty and Slavery	83
30	Gun Control Legislation	99
31	Minuteman Missiles: Scrap Them, Maintain Them, Strengthen Them?	119
	Index	139

Preface

As this book was emerging from successive critiques and revisions, one reviewer deemed it "refreshing" to encounter a prospective publication that "actually accomplishes most of what its creators advertise." If the anonymous reviewer is right, then we have managed not only to assemble study materials that are provocatively topical, but also to use these materials as a means of generating critical sophistication. And if the reviewer is right, then the demands these materials make of students, and of their teachers—demands for close analysis, for sensitivity to subtle distinctions, for constructive skepticism—will prove to be justified.

If the reviewer is right, moreover, then we have managed to justify the demands we have imposed on people who furnished indispensable help toward the creation of this volume. Our list of debts is long. It includes all the authors whose works we have utilized. It most emphatically includes undergraduates at the University of Chicago who submitted patiently, and even enthusiastically, to the crudities of an experimental course in the spring of 1969 called Issues and Arguments in the Social Scientists. A fuller list of our debts is provided in the guide for instructors that accompanies this volume.

We hope the reviewer is right.

John D. May
Redwood City, California
December 1971

Karl J. Bemesderfer
Chicago, Illinois

You go to a great school
not for knowledge as much as for arts and habits;
for the habit of attention, for the art of expression,
for the art of assuming at a moment's notice new intellectual postures,
for the art of entering quickly into another person's thoughts,
for the habit of submitting to censure and refutation,
for the art of indicating assent or dissent in graduated terms,
for the habit of regarding minute points of accuracy,
for the habit of working out what is possible in a given time,
for taste, for discrimination,
for mental courage and mental soberness.
Above all,
you go to a great school for self knowledge.

William Cory, Master of Eton

. . . mistakes are often more illuminating
than are examples of good practice. . . . a diligent
search for errors can serve important functions
in the training of students and in the improvement
of research.

Travis Hirschi and Hannan Selvin

Introduction

Relations between present-day teachers and students seem to be unusually strained. Students accuse their teachers of narrow-mindedness, of hyperfactualism, of neglecting their pedagogical tasks in vulgar pursuit of lush grants for trivial research, of Establishmentarian bias, of disengagement from immediate and urgent problems, of irrelevance. Teachers, in the words of A. M. Tibbetts, find that their students

> ... lack skepticism, and often appear to be able to swallow any generalization on any subject.... They are their own authorities, and ordinarily don't question their right to orate on sociopolitical questions of the greatest moment and complexity. Their typical mode of argument is the unsupported assertion. [They] have not been taught ... that objective facts exist and that there are certain useful methods for investigating and ascertaining them. [They] have not learned how to argue and to express themselves precisely.... [They] have been indoctrinated by their early training to believe that their feelings, emotions, desires, and very beings are the center of the universe.*

This collection of readings and of suggested analytical exercises caters to the more legitimate demands emanating from both camps. It has been marshaled with essentially two aims in mind. First, but hindmost it has been designed to furnish a primitive acquaintance with issues, concepts, questions, proposed answers, proposals, bodies of evidence, and modes of reasoning that characteristically engage the attention of social scientists. Second, but foremost, it has been designed to help students develop critical sophistication. By "critical sophistication" we mean the arts and habits enumerated by William Cory in the epigraph; we mean ability to recognize, and perforce to produce, a well-formed argument, a sound inference, an elegant proof, a plausible explanation, a cogent proposal for remedial action.

*Winter 1968 issue of the *AAUP Bulletin*.

Critical sophistication is an indispensable tool of scientific investigation. It is perhaps peculiarly vital, or peculiarly difficult to sustain, in the several fields of investigation known as "social science," with their complex subject matters, their scarcity of laboratory conditions comparable to those available for work on white rats, their subtle distinctions between disinterested and interested research, their temptations to indulge in wishful thinking, their blurred boundaries separating discovery from advocacy. But at the same time, critical sophistication is vital for all sorts of nonscientific activity. It is the stock in trade of good lawyers. It is a precious asset for businessmen and consumers, who daily confront clashing claims on their limited resources. And it is indispensable for citizens who are endowed with the privilege—and the profound moral obligation—of making authoritative judgments about the performance of their governors.

We can appreciate the usefulness of critical sophistication by reflecting on how frequently we encounter flat assertions of finality. The newspaper columnist, the television pundit, the taxi driver, parents, friends, wise guys, and professors are all inclined to utter the last word on this or that topic, even—or especially—when they do not know enough on which to base the first word. We hear and we frequently believe because we lack the time or the inclination to listen carefully and to go back over the steps supposedly leading from premises to conclusions. Yet most of us can spot hasty transitions and jerry-built arguments. Like other capacities, this one requires exercise for its development. The following pages, we hope, provide such exercises—a regimen, one might say, of mental isometrics.

Our aim is by no means novel. It is implicit in most formulations of the functions of a liberal education. It is explicit in books ostensibly distinguishing between straight and crooked thinking, or elucidating the rhyme of reason or the conduct of inquiry. We have studied many of these books and learned from them, and even pilfered from a few of them. But we have not tried to produce a grand synthesis of these books, which in reality are overlapping, didactic, and rather abstract treatises on deductive and inductive logic, on rhetoric and argumentation, on scientific methods, and on conventional techniques of social research. In a sense, we have devised a supplementary "workbook" for such treatises. In another sense, we have devised an introduction *to* such treatises, because we invite readers to *discover* general principles of reasoning implicit in particular statements as well as to *appreciate* the practicality of mastering such principles. In yet another sense, we have devised an introduction to substantive issues in the several social sciences, because we invite students to recognize stubborn matters of fact on which momentous conclusions depend. But we have not concocted a new cookbook. Instead we have compiled what can be described as a series of *puzzles,* each capable of "solution" (of a sort) within its own terms without *conscious* knowledge of appropriate logical or methodological principles and without special substantive knowledge.

To be more specific, we have assembled some 31 documents that are manifestly addressed to "real world" issues and are eminently "arguable." These documents are distributed among three sections, each dealing with a general class of problems that social scientists and other investigators persistently confront. Most of these documents have the following features:

1. *Brevity*. Students will not be drowned by verbiage, and *will* have time to dissect what they read. The emphasis here is not on imparting information but on helping students to process information.

2. *Topicality*. In the broadest and least vulgar sense students will feel motivated to perform the labors of critical analysis. We call this volume a *working* introduction to social and political inquiry because we tap real statements about real problems.

3. *Analytic adequacy*. Students are in a position to perform definite critical operations. The selected documents are *not* adequate in the sense that they cover any of the topics they address. Accordingly, the readings rarely suffice to enable a rational man to draw sound inferences about the measurement of a given trend, the validity of a proposed explanation, or the propriety of a proposed course of action. Instead, each reading assignment is adequate only in the sense that it contains a *thesis* of some kind, together with a body of allegedly supportive factual and conceptual material. Each reading is adequate or complete in the sense that a student can appraise its thesis *in light of* what its author supplies in the way of evidence and reasoning. Accordingly, students are not precluded from making reasoned judgments by lack of relevant special knowledge about the question at issue. They can be asked to do more than voice agreement or disagreement. We do not, for example, ask students to compare and evaluate clashing versions of the general character of American society (pluralistic or elite dominated?) in which each version has been severed editorially from its allegedly supportive evidence. We do not vaguely exhort readers to "think about" a given problem. Instead, we confront readers with a thesis *and* with its allegedly supportive conceptual and factual premises. We invite readers neither to voice agreement or disagreement with a given thesis nor to judge *ultimate* validity but to assess "fit" between premises and conclusion or conclusions.

4. *Fallibility*. Almost every reading assignment is a case of *poor* "fit" between premises and conclusions. Students are supplied with an initial warning that something is wrong, *palpably* wrong, with a given argument. Accordingly, our basic method of inculcating critical sophistication consists of supplying examples of critical blunders. (However, not every selection conforms to this description. In Exercises 7 and 19, the student is invited to figure out how a plausible inference was reached. In Exercise 31, he is invited to decide which team in the debate made the most persuasive case and why.)

5. *Gradations in the visibility, and variations in the nature, of the blunders*. Some of the mistakes are logical, some statistical, some empirical. Roughly speaking, the puzzles become more difficult as one moves through the book. But this is not invariably the case. Some students have found Exercises 11 and 20 more difficult than subsequent exercises, and Exercise 29 less difficult than many of its predecessors. Moreover, we find little consensus among students as to how the exercises rank in degree of difficulty.

We close this introduction with an expression of bias, of anxiety, and of hope. We are partial to democratic governance. We are anxious—particularly with the advent of suffrage for eighteen year olds—about the current quality of popular judgments and about the current state of efforts by educators to help citizens meet the grave responsibilities that are uniquely theirs in a democratic system of governance. We hope that a better job of citizenship building, rightly understood, can be accomplished; that the techniques used in this volume will contribute to that end; and that other teachers will be stimulated to perfect and augment these techniques.

Our sentiments have been vividly expressed by Suzanne Labin, in an unaccountably neglected book called *The Secret of Democracy* (Vanguard Press, 1955). "Exactly what sort of education," Labin asks, "should the people be given in order to exert genuine control over public affairs?" The people, she replies,

> ... should certainly know more than they know now, but above all, they should know more fundamental things. They should learn to distinguish the sound of truth from that of lies [and] the popular demagogue from the honest reformer, to grasp the frontiers between reality and Utopia, to estimate the hierarchy of dangers, to be open to the objections and aspirations of others, to understand that the shortest path between desires and their realization is tolerance and not dictatorship. . . .
>
> Certainly present-day education falls short of this ideal of popular humanism, which aims at training people's minds rather than at filling them. . . . Let us not forget that education serves to equip minds to control power rather than to exercise it—not to enable men to devise solutions but to choose among those that are offered to them. The *art of thinking* is the essential that everyone should be taught, but not even the elite are taught it today.
>
> . . . It is extremely difficult to teach how to think well, to distinguish hypotheses from certainties and causes from effects, to stick to the subject, to discern what attribute may validly be assigned to a certain subject, to understand that every law has only the finite field of validity imposed by necessity and fruitful approximations, to detect flaws in reasoning, vicious circles, abusive interpolations and extrapolations. It seems possible, nevertheless, at least to teach how to recognize the coarser threads of voluntary or involuntary sophism. . . . The people must be immunized against demagogy, Utopia, or casuistry by systematic exercises in tracking down error, misinterpretation, nonsense, double meaning, evasion, exaggeration, tricks, lies—exercises that must be carried on all one's life outside school. This education would be just as salutary for the elite as for the people.

Section One

Reading Auguries

In ancient Rome men of the highest religious rank were entrusted with the office of auspex or augur. To such men fell the tasks of detecting trends in Roman affairs, of forecasting future events, and of assessing the probable consequences of impending alternative courses of action. Before mighty Caesar sent his legions into battle, he sought the advice of his favorite auspex. This functionary in turn studied the formations disclosed by birds in flight or pondered the entrails of a ritually slaughtered animal. From such "field research" the auspex surmised the propitious moment for commencing a military campaign.

Counterparts of the Roman auspex exist today in every culture. They operate under various names, such as prophet, oracle, diviner, soothsayer, seer. They employ various tools and techniques, such as crystal balls, astrological tables, sacred texts, magic bones cast upon the ground like dice, divining rods, decks of cards, fortune cookies, palmistry, trances, seances, and chants. They are ubiquitous functionaries because they gratify, at least momentarily, our human cravings for guidance and predictability in a world full of perilous uncertainties.

In modern societies much of the work of auguring falls to the lot of applied science. Although the tools of scientists are more reliable than those of ancient augurs, scientific instruments are still manifestly fallible, as we know from experience with weather and election forecasting, oil prospecting, strategic planning, capital investing, medical practice, budgeting, and law making. Costly errors do occur, but sometimes they enable us to refine our investigative techniques.

Endeavors to detect ongoing trends and to identify the probable effects of alternative decisions are fundamentally similar. They consist of deriving a factual inference from a factual premise. The premise is taken to serve as an indicator, or clue, about some matter of immediate concern. The factual inference can prove to be wrong. Errors can emanate from at least three sources: faulty, inappropriate evidence; crude, insufficient evidence; or misconstrued evidence.

The following exercises illustrate modernistic problems of factual inference. The first eight exercises deal with "objective" conditions (trends, behavior, resources). The next seven exercises deal with "subjective" conditions (attitudes, opinions).

In the exercises relating to objective conditions, you are invited to accept the factual evidence pretty much at face value. With the exception of exercise 7, the inferences are of dubious validity in relation to the one or more factual premises. In some cases the inference is clearly untenable, *and* the premise plainly warrants some other inference. In such instances you should identify the reasonable inference, pinpoint the error, and explain your reasoning. In other cases the inference is premature, faulty, or arbitrary, relative to the allegedly supportive factual premise. Here you will be invited to say why the inference is premature, what alternative inference or inferences might be equally plausible, and what additional information would clarify the issue.[1]

In the exercises dealing with subjective conditions, you are exposed not only to pitfalls of interpretation but also to problems having to do with the propriety and the sufficiency of the evidence. Here you come to grips with one of the truly distinctive features of modern society: the public opinion survey. This device is ubiquitous in modern liberal democratic societies, for at least two reasons. First, many kinds of enterprisers, economic and political, realize that their fortunes depend on their success in gratifying the desires of massive publics. These enterprisers need accurate information about public opinions so they can devise attractive products, sales strategies, campaign themes, or legislative programs. They are accordingly prepared to bear the expenses of systematic monitoring. Second,

---

[1] The following statement is an example of a false conclusion drawn from a stated premise, where another conclusion seems warranted: "In 1890, 55.3 percent of the [United States] population fifteen years of age and over was married; in 1920, 59.9 percent was married. There was thus an increase in the population married of 4.6 percent" [William F. Ogburn, "Statistical Studies of Marriage and the Family," in Stuart A. Rice, ed., *Statistics in Social Studies* (Philadelphia: University of Pennsylvania Press, 1930) p. 22]. The conclusion here exemplifies the practice of misconstruing evidence: It confuses percentage change with percentage-*point* change. Actually, an increase of 4.6 percentage *points* (from 53.3 to 59.9) signifies an increase, from the "base" of 55.3, of about 8.3 percent. Moreover, if we want to quibble, we can also challenge the adequacy of the factual evidence. Change in the *total* married population is inferred from change in the proportion of married persons *aged 15 years or older*. There *might* be a significant number of persons, and significant changes in the proportions of persons, under 15 and married.

[2] The following statement is an example of a faulty, premature conclusion: Americans have a sorry record when it comes to participation in elections. Voter turnouts for U.S. presidential elections rarely go as high as 63 percent, as compared with turnouts of 75–90 percent for national elections in Canada, Britain, the Commonwealth democracies, and Western European nations (Paraphrased from a statement by Morris Udall in the *Congressional Record*, 13 August 1970, p. H8319). The conclusion (a "sorry" United States record on electoral participation) is faulty—but not necessarily wrong, in the final analysis—for a number of reasons. First, it arbitrarily presupposes that high turnouts are good. Second, it infers electoral participation rates solely from rates of turnout at national general elections. There could be many *other* elections, and participation in these might be such that *cumulative* rates of electoral participation, per adult citizen per year, are *higher* in the U.S. than elsewhere. Finally, the figures are meaningless. The statement speaks of "turnouts" of 63 and 75 "percent" but does not answer the question "percent of whom?" In one case the figure *might* be based on total population, or on total adult population; whereas in another case the figure *might* be based on adults legally eligible to vote, or on those registered to vote.

they cannot readily meet the demand for accurate information about public opinions by holding an infinite number of general referendums because of prohibitive costs and increasingly unreliable results as rates of participation declined. Consequently, although people in modern societies do not troop incessantly to the polls, pollsters troop incessantly to the people.

But pollsters rarely try to contact all the people who belong to target groups. Such coverage is physically and economically impossible, at least where the target group consists of American consumers or the American electorate. For example, George Gallup's American Institute of Public Opinion customarily infers the political sentiments of the American electorate at large—close to 100 million people—from queries actually posed to about 1500 respondents. Gallup stoutly maintains, and most professional social scientists agree, that such a tiny fraction of responses *can* suffice to disclose the views of a massive public. Sample *size* is just one consideration in deciding whether a given opinion survey is *representative* and hence *reliable*. Many issues revolve around the matter of representativeness.

Additional problems engage the attention of opinion researchers. Questions may inadvertently induce respondents to give replies that delude interviewers about respondents' true feelings. Respondents may more consciously mislead interviewers. Interviewers may consciously or unconsciously emit cues that yield misleading records of respondents' feelings. Opinions can undergo abrupt change—as they apparently did on a large scale in late October 1948, after the professional pollsters believed "conclusively" that Dewey would beat Truman in the presidential election. Moreover, counting errors can occur.

Exercises 9 through 13 present opportunities for critical comment on the "fit" between an interpretation of what a given opinion survey discloses and a description of the conduct of that survey. Exercises 14 and 15 present opportunities for participation in disputes about the reliability of pollsters' election forecasts.

Objective Conditions

Exercise 1. Location of a Safe Haven

During the Spanish-American War, statistical evidence indicated that the death rate among members of the United States Navy was 9 per 1,000, while the death rate among inhabitants of New York City was 16 per 1,000. Such data prompted a New York publisher to claim that the Navy was a safer place than Fun City.

Your assignment is to state, concisely, why the publisher's inference is premature. In other words, indicate why the evidence, regardless of its accuracy, is not sufficient to sustain a reliable comparison between the Navy and New York City in terms of hazards to life. Could New York City have a higher death rate and still have a "safer" environment?

Exercise 2. Effectiveness in Law Enforcement

At a hearing before a committee of the United States Senate some time ago, the following dialogue was recorded:

> *Mr. Bennett:* The number of men in prison today, if you put together all the State prisons and all the Federal prisons, is less than it was just prior to the war. That means, it seems to me, that we are doing a better job of law enforcement all the way through.
> *Mr. Levi:* Would you say that that means that crime is on the decrease?
> *Mr. Bennett:* If you can measure crime in terms of the men who go to prison, I think it is. . . .

Your assignment is to identify some alternative interpretations of the finding that the United States prison population has declined.

Exercise 3. Electoral Participation

In the *Congressional Record* of August 13, 1970, Representative Morris Udall delivered the following remarks:

> The number of non-voters [in the United States] is increasing at an average over the last decade of one million each year, [or] four million each presidential election. [Such a trend shows that] somewhere along the line we failed to take adequate notice and provide intelligent remedies for the increasingly serious problem of non-voting. [Moreover, the trend figures show that, despite various "technological advances," which "should facilitate voter participation,"] the political participation of Americans has not increased, it has declined.

Your assignment is to assess the plausibility of the conclusion that "the political participation of Americans . . . has declined" in relation to the factual premise supplied in this statement. Can an increase in number of nonvoters occur along with an increase in total "political participation"?

Exercise 4. Medical Progress

A journal commented editorially that "age-specific death rates from breast cancer have remained constant for 35 years. This constancy indicates that no significant advances in methods of treatment of breast cancer have been made."
Age-specific death rates are obtained by dividing the number of deaths by the number of women in a specified age group. An example of "constancy" would be if 13 out of every 1000 fatalities among women between the age of 35 and 45 resulted from breast cancer in the years 1940, 1945, 1950, 1955, 1960, 1965, and 1970.

Your assignment is to discuss whether, and to what extent, the constancy in age-specific death rates does plausibly indicate that indeed no significant advances in methods of treating this malady have occurred. Could the factual premise be true and the inference false? How?

Exercise 5. The Spread of Knowledge

Americans readily believe that individual well-being and social progress depend directly on the extent to which many people spend many years in high-quality schools. Accordingly, they are anxious to know whether they and their fellow citizens are becoming more or less educated. The following extract from a magazine embodies one approach to measurement:

> In spite of all our effort at education, the American people are becoming more ignorant. . . . Women college graduates, aged 45–49, have had barely half enough children to replace their parents; high school graduates, same age, four-fifths enough children for replacement. . . . *But* women, same age, with fourth grade education or less, have had nearly twice the number necessary to replace the parents. Fourth-graders are practically doubling their numbers every generation; college women are dying out 50 percent every generation.

Your assignment is to discuss the propriety of the first sentence in the quoted passage in light of the information provided in the succeeding sentences. Does the evidence provided warrant this thesis? If not, why?

Exercise 6. Defense Capabilities

In his syndicated newspaper column a few years back, Joseph Alsop discussed the probable effectiveness of a contemplated complex of defense barriers against attacking aircraft. He estimated that if the probability of knocking down an attacking aircraft were 0.15 at each of five sets of barriers (equipped with radar and intercepting aircraft) and if the attacker had to pass all five barriers to reach its target, then the probability of success in knocking down the attacker before it passed all five barriers would be 0.75.

Your assignment is (1) to assess Alsop's estimate in relation to the given premise, and (2) if you feel his estimate is incorrect, to provide a more accurate estimate, explaining your reasoning. (You might find it useful to conduct a war game on paper, starting with 100 attack planes.)

Exercise 7. Cheating on Examinations

On March 12, 1966, 223 men took a civil service examination in search of jobs as operating engineers for the Sanitary District of Chicago. Fifteen jobs needed to be filled immediately. The minimum passing grade was 70. The scores were reported to Vinton W. Bacon, superintendent of the Sanitary District. After looking over the reported results, Bacon declared, in effect, "I smell a rat!" Subsequent investigation confirmed that the reported results did not honestly reflect individual performances on the examination. The list of reported scores that aroused Bacon's suspicions was as follows:

26,27,27,27,27   29,30,30,30,30   31,31,31,32,32   33,33,33,33,33
34,34,34,35,35   36,36,36,37,37   37,37,37,37,37   39,39,39,39,39
39,39,40,41,42   42,42,42,42,43   43,43,43,43,43   43,43,44,44,44
44,44,44,45,45   45,45,45,45,45   46,46,46,46,46   46,47,47,47,47
47,47,48,48,48   48,48,48,48,48   49,49,49,49,50   50,51,51,51,51

51,52,52,52,52   52,53,53,53,53   53,54,54,54,54   54,55,55,55,56
56,56,56,56,57   57,57,57,58,58   58,58,58,58,58   58,59,59,59,59
60,60,60,60,60   60,61,61,61,61   61,61,62,62,62   63,63,64,65,66
66,66,67,67,67   67,68,68,69,69   69,69,69,69,69   69,71,71,72,73
74,74,74,75,75   76,76,78,80,80   80,80,81,81,81   82,82,83,83,83

83,84,84,84,84   84,84,84,90,90   90,91,91,91,92   92,92,93,93,93
93,95,95

Your assignment is to explain why Bacon suspected cheating (by certain examinees, by testers, by the reporters of results) on the basis of this set of figures. (If the "solution" does not come to mind in the course of, *say*, half an hour of thought, you might experiment with ways of depicting the distribution of test scores graphically.)

Exercise 8. Gauging Quality Control

In a firm manufacturing widgets the managers found that they had to expect about 5 percent of the units made to be defective but that the rate need never exceed 10 percent with good materials, machines properly adjusted, and skillful workmanship. One week, however, more than 10 percent of the widgets produced were reported to be defective, so the next week special care was given to restoring quality. Nevertheless, 16.4 percent of the widgets made that week were reported to be defective. The inspectors' records contained the following tabulations:

	Units inspected	Units defective	Percent defective
Monday	70	0	0
Tuesday	68	2	3.0
Wednesday	68	3	4.4
Thursday	70	1	1.4
Friday	72	4	5.5
Saturday	32	1	3.1
Totals	380	11	16.4

The production managers held a meeting. They decided that the snafu was not in the production line so much as in the accounting. But they disagreed about the actual rate of production of defective units among those inspected during the week. One manager said the correct figure was 18.4 percent, another said 17.4 percent, another said 3.45 percent, another said 3.12 percent, another said 3.1 percent, another said 3.05 percent, another said 3.015 percent, another said 2.895 percent, another said 2.73 percent—and the office boy said they were all wrong.

Your assignment is (1) to name the correct figure (percent of defective widgets for the week) and explain how you arrived at it, and (2) to suggest how the other figures probably were reached and explain what was wrong with the procedures used.

Subjective Conditions

Exercise 9.   Student Opinion on Homework Loads

A college newspaper campaigning in favor of shorter homework assignments sought to probe student opinion on the subject. Ballots were printed in the newspaper, and participants in the survey were asked to bring the ballots to the newspaper office, which was located in a remote corner of the campus. Ballots amounting to one fourth of the enrolled students were cast, and almost four-fifths of these ballots recorded sentiments in favor of shorter assignments, according to the newspaper's editors. The editors claimed that the proposal was overwhelmingly popular among the students.

Your assignment is to list reasons for questioning the newspaper staff's interpretation of student opinion, on the basis of the described survey.

Exercise 10.   Community Opinion on Tax Reform

Congressman Homer Claghorn commissioned an opinion survey to learn his constituents' feelings about a proposed increase in the federal income tax exemption for children. The survey organization adopted this plan: Certain neighborhoods were singled out so that each geographical section and each economic level in the district would be "represented." Interviewers made a door-to-door canvass in the selected neighborhoods. They canvassed from 9 A.M. to noon, from Monday through Saturday, during the first three weeks of January. When nobody responded when the canvasser rang a given door, the canvasser crossed that household off his list.

The persons interviewed voiced overwhelming support for the increased tax exemption. As a result, Claghorn concluded that the measure was overwhelmingly popular among his constituents.

Your assignment is to discuss the propriety of Claghorn's conclusion in light of the procedures used and the results described.

Exercise 11. Community Opinion on Busing

A civil rights organization desired to discover the opinions of white and black citizens on whether school children should be transported on buses within a given district to achieve racial balance in the public schools. Interviewers went into both black and white neighborhoods, with the following results: White respondents indicated opposition to busing by a margin of 5 to 1; black respondents were evenly divided on the question. The sponsors of the survey, disturbed by the results, decided to resurvey the neighborhoods. They employed another polling organization for this work and instructed the group to use exactly the same question that had been asked six weeks earlier. This time the results showed white respondents evenly divided, whereas black respondents favored busing by a margin of 6 to 1.

Your assignment is to suggest factors that might explain this striking divergence.

Exercise 12. Community Opinion on "Escalation"

In March 1970, Congressman Claghorn decided to ascertain his constituents' feelings about United States operations in Indo-China. The polling expert announced in April that two thirds of Claghorn's constituents favored "escalation" of United States military activities in Indo-China. This assessment was inferred from a survey conducted in the following manner: Every twenty-fifth name in the telephone directory covering the Congressional district was copied onto a slip of paper. Each paper, identical in size, weight, and color to the others, was put into a barrel. After the papers had been mixed thoroughly, a blindfolded child picked out 350 papers. The pollster interviewed every available person from among the 350. He asked each respondent, "Do you favor escalation of United States military activities in Indo-China?" Affirmative answers outnumbered negative answers by a margin of 2 to 1.

Your assignment is to discuss the propriety of the pollster's inference that two thirds of Claghorn's constituents favor "escalation" in light of the findings previously described. These questions may prove helpful: Did the method of selecting a *sample* of potential respondents yield a *representative* subgroup of the target population? Was the *canvassing* procedure reliable? Was the *question* posed to respondents adequate for the intended purpose? What *kinds* of answers might be given to this question?

Exercise 13. Change in Community Opinion on "Escalation"

In June 1970, Congressman Claghorn again sponsored an opinion survey on "escalation," addressed to the same persons who responded in the earlier survey. Each original respondent was contacted again. This time, affirmative and negative answers were evenly divided.

Your assignment is to state whether any reliable inferences can be drawn from

Subjective Conditions

these two sets of findings, even if there is substantial reason to doubt the meaningfulness of the original survey as a measure of constituents' attitudes. If such an inference can be drawn, state it precisely.

Exercise 14. Testing for Poll Reliability: Prediction Versus Actuality

A popular way of assessing the reliability of opinion surveys and of comparing polling organizations consists of comparing predicted results with actual results. This means was used to determine the reasons for the public's rejection of the Edsel automobile. It is more commonly used, under the glare of massive publicity, in assessing the outcomes of presidential elections.

In 1960 Senator Albert Gore of Tennessee entered in the Congressional Record an exchange of correspondence he had initiated with pollsters George Gallup and Elmo Roper. Gore raised questions about the accuracy of the Gallup and Roper polls in reflecting the true state of public opinion as the measurable difference between predicted and actual electoral results indicated. Gallup defended the accuracy of his poll thus:

> Since 1948—when many basic changes in polling procedures were instituted—the average deviation from absolute accuracy of the Gallup poll in five national elections—1950, 1952, 1954, 1956, and 1958—has been 1.7 percentage points, as the following table shows:

Popular vote	Gallup poll	Election returns	Deviation of poll (percentage points)
National			
1950 congressional	51% Democratic	50.3% Democratic	0.7
1952 presidential	51% Eisenhower	55.4% Eisenhower	4.4
1954 congressional	51.5% Democratic	52.7% Democratic	1.2
1956 presidential	59.5% Eisenhower	57.8% Eisenhower	1.7
1958 congressional	57% Democratic	56.5% Democratic	.5
Outside the South			
1950 congressional	48.5% Democratic	47.3% Democratic	1.2
1954 congressional	48.5% Democratic	49.5% Democratic	1.0
1958 congressional	54% Democratic	53.9% Democratic	.1
Average deviation for five national elections			1.7
Average deviation for three estimates, outside the South			.8

> In the seven national elections up to and including 1948, the average deviation was 3.9 percentage points.
>
> If you take all twelve national elections—every election since we started in 1936—the average deviation would be 3 percentage points.

Gore found the table and the accompanying remarks unconvincing as evidence of substantial accuracy in presidential opinion polls. He suggested that

Gallup's emphasis on "percentage point deviation" served to underestimate the size of error in predicting results.

Your assignment is to indicate the grounds for Gore's suggestion that the size of error in prediction is somewhat larger than what Gallup's data on "deviation" suggests.

Exercise 15. Quality of Responses

In another part of his letter to Gore, George Gallup included a card containing the exact form of words and layout that his interviewers used for Presidential preference polls. Gore responded to this information by running the following experiment:

> In an effort to test polls and polling methods, five people from my staff gave a Saturday of their time and conducted a poll of the city of Washington, using an exact duplicate of Dr. Gallup's poll card except that we supplied the names of the persons on the card. They followed as best they could a scientific method, except that on the basis of Dr. Gallup's standard sample, they polled about 18 times as many as Dr. Gallup would have normally allotted to an area with the population of the District of Columbia. We chose Saturday because this was a time when it could be expected that men as well as women would be at their homes.
>
> Those polled were given a choice of cards marked either Republican or Democratic, and if a respondent were an independent, he was given a Democratic card to mark. In a total sample of 182 participants, 120 took Democratic cards and 62 selected Republican cards.
>
> For the purposes of this experiment, the Democratic card contained the following names, in the order listed:
>
> 1. Allen Dulles
> 2. John D. Eisenhower
> 3. Hubert Humphrey
> 4. Lyndon Johnson
> 5. Thomas Jefferson Jones
> 6. John F. Kennedy
> 7. Franklin D. Roosevelt, Jr.
> 8. Adlai Stevenson
> 9. Stuart Symington
>
> All four major geographical divisions of Washington were polled, generally on the basis of their proportionate population. Of those taking a Democratic card, 25 percent listed either Franklin D. Roosevelt, Jr., or John D. Eisenhower as their preference for either first or second place. That was on the Democratic ticket.
>
> The results in Southwest Washington—the first area polled—were even more striking. Since this is the smallest geographical division, the sample used there was the smallest taken. Here John D. Eisenhower ran second for the Democratic presidential nomination, being nosed out of a tie by only one ballot. Of the 22 persons responding to the Democratic card, 6, or 27 percent, chose the familiar Eisenhower

name as either their first or second choice. The son, Franklin D. Roosevelt, Jr., of a former famous President, however, topped him in total first and second place selections by getting 9 votes, or 41 percent.

Since names of several of my colleagues were included, I will not go further in announcing the results of this trial heat in the interest of comity in the Senate. Moreover, I would not want to risk the possibility of influencing anyone by revealing the results at this time.

Your assignment is to indicate what, if anything, Gore's experiment shows or strongly indicates and what criticisms, if any, we may make of it. These questions may prove helpful: What does "name familiarity" mean to a voter or to a candidate or to a pollster? Under what conditions can one infer voting intention or actual voting from "name familiarity"?

Section Two

Sorting Out Causes and Effects

An entomologist who sought to learn how grasshoppers hear proceeded by exposing a group of typical grasshoppers to the sound of a whistle. All the grasshoppers hopped. He then amputated the legs of half the grasshoppers. At the next sound of the whistle, all of the nonamputees hopped again, while none of the amputees hopped. His conclusion was that grasshoppers hear with their legs.

A man found that he got uncomfortably drunk on a quart of scotch mixed with a quart of water, so he changed to a similar quantity of bourbon and water. He still got drunk, so he changed to rye and water. He again got drunk, so he changed to brandy and water. At this point, applying his common sense to the plainest facts at his disposal, he decided to quit drinking water.

A chemist compounded a new substance, which, he suspected, would cure the common cold. He tried the compound on hundreds of cold sufferers, and 97 percent completely recovered within two weeks. The other 3 percent proved to be afflicted with ailments incorrectly diagnosed as colds. The chemist concluded that at last he had found the sovereign remedy for the common cold.

An inventor applied for a patent on a tiger repellent. The inventor certified that he had used the repellent for 23 years on his apartment and on the apartments of his neighbors in Manhattan, and not one tiger had crossed a treated threshold. Thus he concluded that the tiger repellent is highly effective.

More recently a prominent law enforcement official reviewed evidence indicating, beyond a reasonable doubt, that every heroin addict previously had been a marijuana smoker. His conclusion was that "marijuana use leads to heroin use."

One of the foregoing stories exemplifies an inference that, on the strength of established knowledge, we can confidently deem *false*. Every one of the stories exemplifies an inference that we can confidently deem *faulty*. Each example—

like some of the exercises in Section One—illustrates the practice of jumping to conclusions, or deriving an inference about cause and effect from insufficient and/or inappropriate evidence. Can you state why each inference is faulty? Can you suggest further tests of probable validity? Can you formulate generalizations about the *kinds* of experimental and/or analytical blunders depicted in these stories? If so, you are prepared to appreciate, if not to participate in, the principal work of science. Sorting out the various causes of various effects is, to a large extent, the daily business of scientists. The work of investigation, of testing hunches about cause and effect, requires a high degree of subject matter specialization. Yet the rules or principles concerning inference are universal.

The exercises in this section provide additional examples of assertions about cause and effect. The examples, drawn from a variety of topics engaging the attention of social scientists, generally involve faulty inferences. On the basis of the evidence your task is to identify which causal inferences are warranted and which unwarranted, and to state the bases for your choices.

Juvenile Delinquency

Until recently, with the advent of hippies, dropouts, and student "militants," when adults fretted about youth they commonly alluded to juvenile delinquency. Substantial resources were devoted to probing rates and sources of, and ostensible remedies for, juvenile delinquency. The numerous studies have yielded abundant examples of durable problems in the broader field of social causation. Here are some examples.

Exercise 16. Race?

Some investigations have disclosed a positive statistical relation between the rates of juvenile delinquency in various neighborhoods (indicated by police and court records) and the ethnic composition of these neighborhoods. Specifically, the evidence indicates that rates of juvenile delinquency are abnormally high in neighborhoods where proportions of non-Caucasians are abnormally high. Let us imagine that on the basis of these statistical correlations Professor Bilbo declares that objective evidence proves that criminal tendencies are peculiarly ingrained in non-Caucasians.

Your assignment is to suggest reasons for regarding Professor Bilbo's inference, on the basis of the evidence mentioned here, as an example of jumping to conclusions.

Exercise 17. Bad Company?

A common theory about the source of juvenile delinquency involves "differential association." And a common version of such a theory suggests that certain youngsters become delinquent because they associate with other youngsters who already are delinquent. But this explanation, like so many others, has frequently been attacked, the charge being that it confounds incidental effects with causes.

In a widely renowned study involving 500 delinquent boys from the Boston area and 500 nondelinquent boys of similar background, 98.4 percent of the delinquents and only 7.4 percent of the nondelinquents were found to have delinquent friends. The significance of this finding was subject to dispute between those arguing that "birds of a feather flock together."

Your assignment is to suggest the nature of *additional information* that would clarify the character (causal, noncausal) of the reported statistical association. In other words what kind of evidence would indicate that deliquency comes from associating with delinquents? What evidence would discredit that theory?

Exercise 18.   Bad and Older Company?

According to the authors of the beforementioned study, "The delinquents not only chummed largely with other delinquents but [also] gravitated toward older boys." Specifically, 44.6 percent of the delinquents in their sample of 500 delinquent boys associated with predominantly older boys, whereas 33.8 percent associated with boys approximately their own age, 4.4 percent associated with predominantly younger boys, and 17.2 percent associated with companions of diverse ages.

From this information a reviewer derived the following alternative conclusions: (a) the 500 youths in this study did not constitute a representative sample of juvenile delinquents; (b) although the sample was representative, the data here are not to be trusted; or (c) in any case it would be absurd to ascribe juvenile delinquency to association with older delinquent companions.

Your assignment is to explain how such conclusions could reasonably be reached.

Exercise 19.   Family Size and Birth Order?

If the proposition that parental neglect of children encourages juvenile delinquency contains any truth, then there might be some additional truth to the propositions that juvenile delinquency is a function of being from a large family (each child being liable to neglect because of the competition) and/or of being a "middle" child (first-born and youngest children being the most likely targets of parental care).

An investigation designed to test the latter propositions, using "matching" sets of delinquent and nondelinquent boys, yielded the following figures:

Number of Children in Family by Delinquency

	Delinquents		Nondelinquents		Difference
	number	%	number	%	
1 child	24	4.8	43	8.6	−3.8%
2 children	29	5.8	62	12.4	−6.6
3 children	46	9.2	61	12.2	−3.0
4 children	71	14.2	76	15.2	−1.1
5 children	66	13.2	74	14.8	−1.6
6 children	78	15.6	48	9.6	6.0
7 children	72	14.4	49	9.8	4.6
8 children or more	114	22.8	87	17.4	5.5
Totals	500	100	500	100	

Rank of Boy among Siblings by Delinquency

	Delinquents		Nondelinquents		Difference
	number	%	number	%	
Only child	24	4.8	43	8.6	−3.8
First born	78	15.6	97	19.4	−3.8
Middle	300	60	239	47.8	12.2
Youngest	98	19.6	121	24.2	−4.6
Totals	500	100	500	100	

Your assignment is to rationalize the following assessment of the foregoing figures: "Although the data show a positive association between family bigness and delinquency, and another positive association between birth order (being a 'middle' child) and delinquency, it is almost certain that the latter association is spurious. Middle-order birth probably is not a cause of delinquency."

"Athleticism" and Neurosis

Physical fitness—like liberty, motherhood, and fair play—seems to be one of those causes above dispute. During his brief term in office, President John F. Kennedy identified himself vividly with the cause of keeping fit physically by regular exercise. His political adversaries did not accuse him of advocating a cause that was inherently reprehensible. But surely there is room for argument about the value of physical fitness or about the value of *emphasis* on physical fitness. Perhaps people can be concerned with physical fitness to the detriment of themselves or their communities.

Exercise 20. What *TIME* Said Doctor Little Said

An article in the January 12, 1970, issue of *TIME* voiced the possibility that concern with physical fitness can be detrimental. The text of the article was as follows:

How To Be Fit But Neurotic*

He is as healthy as a hound dog. He lifts weights, jogs, does push-ups, plays squash on his lunch hour and likes to get out there with the kids and make like Joe Namath. Yet, in his prolonged obsession with physical prowess, the middle-aged fitness fanatic may be exceptionally vulnerable to mental illness.

This somewhat unsettling conclusion was reached by Scottish Psychiatrist J. Crawford Little after analyzing the cases of 72 neurotic male patients. Among 44 men who were intensely concerned with their athletic ability, Little reports in the journal *Acta Psychiatrica Scandinavica,* 32 suffered from neuroses that had been set off by physical ailments. Often they were trifling, such as a sprained ankle or a bout of flu. Of 28 nonathletic neurotics, however, only three had mental problems that could be traced at least partially to physical sources. Most of the athletic patients had been fit all their lives and had had happy childhoods, successful marriages and stable personal relationships. But, Little says, "they were overinvolved with physical fitness and health and had come to value them very highly." Thus, in their late 30s and early 40s, when strength started to deteriorate, the athletic patients had become very sensitive to their physical condition.

"This kind of man," says Little, "needs only a slight illness to trigger off a serious neurosis that often lasts for years and is very difficult to cure. The most valuable thing in life—his fitness—has been taken away, and he can't fill the gap." Most of Little's nonathletic patients could take physical illness in stride. Their neuroses had more familiar origins: problems in marriage or work.

How can health buffs protect themselves against middle age neurosis? Little, who is 47 and confines his exercise to the mild seasonal Scottish sport of curling (a kind of bowling on ice), suggests that they take up painting or rose growing—almost any avocation other than strenuous athletics. "Unless he has something else to fall back on," the psychiatrist warns, "a man playing hockey or football beyond the age of 42 is asking for trouble."

Your assignment is to comment critically, concisely, and constructively on this *TIME* piece. What views, precisely, are imputed to Doctor Little? In what manner and to what extent does the evidence ascribed to Doctor Little bear on the causal inference(s) and the advice ascribed to Doctor Little?

Exercise 21. What Doctor Little Said

TIME's four paragraphs on "How To Be Fit But Neurotic" came from a 35-paragraph, statistically lavish article in a journal devoted to psychiatric research. The text of the original article is reprinted on pages 18–27.

Your assignment is first, to assess, on the basis of the *TIME* piece and Doctor

*Reprinted by permission from *TIME,* The Weekly Newsmagazine; Copyright Time Inc.

Little's original article, (1) the accuracy of TIME's version of Little's immediate findings and (2) the propriety of TIME's version of Little's conclusions (factual and practical) and second, to assess the fit between Little's evidence and his conclusions. In referring to "TIME's version of Little's immediate findings," bear in mind primarily the information contained in paragraphs 2 and 3 of "How To Be Fit But Neurotic." In referring to "TIME's version of Little's conclusions (factual and practical)," consider the statements in paragraphs 1 and 4 of "How To Be Fit But Neurotic."

In social science a generalization shown to be true of more than one group of subjects is stronger than one established for only a single experimental group. Thus, if we were to find that New Yorkers, Chicagoans and Londoners suffered some hearing loss compared to residents of quiet farmlands, the evidence would be stronger for an association between urban living and hearing loss than it would be if we simply acquired such data for one city. Each time we were to find similar results in a new city, our confidence in the generalization would increase. And if the results were to persist with urban and rural residents matched in terms of personal traits, such as sex, age, and body type, the generalization would gain still more plausibility.

In a similar way, Little appears to have studied various groups of respondents — neurotics and non-neurotics, "athletics" and non-"athletics." How consistent are the various comparisons with one another? Do the statistical associations tend to support a generalization about "athleticism" and neurosis or do they contradict one another?

J. Crawford Little

The Athlete's Neurosis — A Deprivation Crisis*

I. Athleticism

I. 2. In the clinical investigation of a series of seventy-two male neurotic patients, referred to a general hospital psychiatric clinic and to private practice over the years 1959–62 in an industrial city in Northern England (Leeds, population 520,000), it was found that these neurotic subjects fell into two extreme categories with respect to "athleticism," i.e. their personal valuation of physical prowess. On the one hand were the thirty-nine percent who appeared, to the exclusion of other interests, to overvalue health and fitness, revealing an inordinate pride in their previous sickness-free progress through life and in their excess physical stamina, strength or skill. In complete contrast were the forty-two per-

*Reprinted by permission from Acta Psychiatrica Scandinavica, vol. 45, no. 2, pp. 187–97. Copyright 1969 Munksgaard, Ltd. All rights reserved.

cent of the neurotic series who had shown an almost complete lack of awareness of physical wellbeing throughout life and had never shown the slightest interest in sport, games, athletics or other physical activities.

I. 2. The two groups were categorised male neurotics of (a) athletic personality ("athletic neurotics") and (b) non-athletic personality ("non-athletic neurotics").

I. 3. It was evident that such extreme variance with respect to athleticism was uncommon in a group of non-neurotic male control subjects matched with the neurotic subjects for age, social class and family doctor interviewed in their homes in Leeds in 1965, for seventy-two percent of the controls, but only eighteen

Table 1. Athleticism

	N	Grade +2 (Extremely athletic attitudes and practices)	Grades +1, 0, −1 ('Normal' athletic attitudes and practices)	Grade −2 (Completely non-athletic attitudes and practices)	Total
Consecutive series of male neurotic patients (1964)	33	13 (39%)	6 (18%)	14 (42%)	33 (99%)
Normal male controls matched for age (1965)	33	3 (9%)	24 (72%)	6 (18%)	33 (99%)

χ^2 (Yates correction) 17.146. df.2. $p < 0.001$.

percent of the neurotic subjects, revealed attitudes and had followed practices with respect to physical prowess appropriate to their age. Only nine percent of controls, compared with thirty-nine percent of neurotics, were classified as "athletic personalities."

I. 4. Table 1 and Figure 1 show the essentially dichotomous distribution of the personality variable "athleticism" in neurotic males.

I. 5. Although "athleticism" may appear a somewhat nebulous and subjective concept, nevertheless independent psychiatrists' rating on a five point scale of this personality variable disclosed a high degree of interobserver agreement. (product moment correlation, $r = +.93$).

II. Comparison of Athletic and Non-Athletic Neurotic Males

II. 1. Statistically significant differences emerged in the detailed comparison of the two groups with respect to (A) the circumstances surrounding the onset of the neurotic illness, (B) the nature of the illness itself, and (C) the premorbid aspects of personality and life experience.

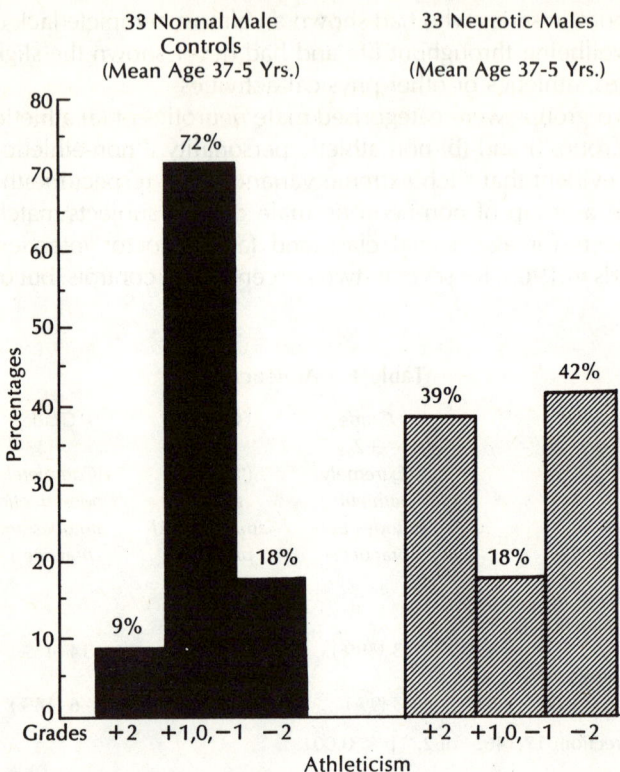

Figure 1. The distribution of athleticism as a personality variable in male neurotics and controls

(A) *Onset*

(1) *Age*

II. 2. Table 2 shows the mean age difference between the two neurotic groups at the time of onset of symptoms and at the time of psychiatric referral.

(2) *The apparent precipitant*

II. 3. In the forty-four athletic subjects a direct threat to their own physical well-being, in the form of illness or injury, had initiated the neurotic breakdown in 72.5 percent of cases, while in the twenty-eight neurotics of non-athletic per-

Table 2. Age

	Male neurotics			
	Athletic personality		Non-athletic personality	
	N	Mean age	N	Mean age
Age at onset of the neurotic illness	44	36.36 years	28	29.32 years	t test P < .01
Age at referral to psychiatrist	44	40.3 years	28	34.61 years	t test P < .05

sonality such physical threats had preceded the onset of symptoms in only 10.7 percent—a highly significant difference as shown in Table 3.

II. 4. Thus, it can be seen that male neurotics of athletic personality displayed a striking stressor/vulnerability specificity; the men became exquisitely vulnerable, on approaching the fifth decade of life, to threats to their overvalued but *waning* physical prowess, and were relatively insensitive to other types of stressor. Conversely, in non-athletic male neurotics, with their low valuation of physical prowess, only rarely did a physical threat initiate the neurotic symptomatology. The findings reemphasize that an apparently trivial stressor can be a major crisis for an individual, only comprehensible to an observer who has assessed the subject's valuation/vulnerability system.

Table 3. Direct threat to physical wellbeing—Male neurotics

	Present exclusively	Present with other psychological stressors	Not present	Total
Athletic neurotics	23 (52%)	9 (20.5%)	12 (27.5%)	44 (100%)
Non-athletic neurotics	2 (7%)	1 (3.5%)	25 (89.5%)	28 (100%)

χ^2 (Yates correction) 22.75   2 df.   p < .001.

II. 5. The neurotic symptoms developed in the great majority of the athletic subjects almost immediately following injury, and in many cases, indeed on the same day. Where a physical illness preceded the neurosis, the symptoms of the former became perpetuated and exaggerated along with the emergence of further neurotic symptoms. Rarely was there a symptom-free period between the physical assault and the onset of the neurosis. In most cases the physical assault was a relatively minor one of the sort which must be fairly common in men of this age; it would appear that the magnitude of the vulnerability is more critical than the intensity of the immediate traumatic experience, in which area *relevance* is the conspicuous characteristic.

II. 6. Physical assaults immediately preceded the onset of neurotic maladjustment in thirty-two of the forty-four subjects of athletic premorbid personality; details are as follows:

II. 7. *Major physical stress — 8 cases:* Osteotomy; coronary thrombosis; fractured spine, femur and foot; fractured femur; bronchogenic carcinoma; severe leg wound; acute rheumatoid arthritis; pulmonary T. B.

II. 8. *Moderate physical stress — 6 cases:* In 3 cases the stressors were cumulative with eruption of neurotic symptomatology following the final trauma. In 3 cases the stress was single:

Cumulative stresses (3)	3 cumulative events: sciatica-lumbago, diagnosis of prolapsed intervertebral disc, *dental pain;* 4 cumulative events: dental extraction, fractured metacarpal, serious dog bite, *attack of sinuitis;* 3 cumulative events: injury to testicle, hydrocele, *operation on hydrocele.*
Single stress (3)	Hospitalisation with suspected coronary thrombosis; concussion; hospitalisation with renal infection and prolapsed intervertebral disc.

II. 9. *Minor physical stresses — 17 cases:* Injury to ankle; attack of lumbago; development of hernia; influenza (3 cases); advice to have surgery for benign parotid tumour; acute awareness of rapid loss of fitness for much-loved active sports; febrile illness; mild encephalitis; two episodes on hockey field: blow on back from ball, and collision with another player; hurt back when lifting at work; feeling no longer strong enough for heavy job; P. U. O.; hypertension revealed by G. P.; several minor injuries on the rugby field; onset of perceptive deafness and tinnitus in the right ear; strained back muscles.

II. 10. *Indirect physical stress — 1 case:* This patient, a very keen footballer, fainted in the cinema at the moment in the film ("Reach for the Sky") when the hero's legs (Bader) are to be amputated. An intractable depersonalization state immediately ensued.

Total 32 cases.

II. 11. In nine of these athletic subjects with an apparent physical precipitant, there was *in addition* psychological stress of a non-physical nature present at the onset or shortly before.

II. 12. In 12 only (27.5 percent) of the 44 male neurotics judged to have athletic personalities was there absence of a precipitating stress with a component of physical insult. The comparable figures for the male neurotics with non-athletic personalities were 25 out of 28 cases (89.5 percent).

II. 13. In the *non-athletic* subjects three types of stressor were associated with the onset of neurosis in 60 percent of the subjects, viz.: difficulties arising from rigid attitudes at work, marital disruption and sexual problems, and death or illness in members of the family group or in friends.

II. 14. It is of interest that in the entire series of seventy-two neurotic males (athletic and non-athletic combined) in only thirteen percent was the neurotic illness apparently precipitated by sexual or marital difficulties, while bereavement and illness in family and friends preceded the onset in twice as many.

(B) *Nosology*

II. 15. The ensuing neurotic disorders in the athletic subjects were in the main clinically indistinguishable from those seen in the non-athletic subjects, being predominantly anxiety and reactive depressive syndromes. Certain manifesta-

Table 4

	Male neurotics				Y = Yates correction applied	df	P
	With athletic personality		With non-athletic personality				
	N		N		χ^2		
1. Family history of minor psychiatric illness	41	8 (19.5%)	27	13 (48%)	6.25	—	1	<.02
2. Absence of any known psychiatric illness in the family	41	26 (63%)	27	9 (34%)	5.9	—	1	<.02
3. "Good" relationship with mother	44	33 (75%)	28	12 (43%)	7.54	—	1	<.01
4. "Good" relationship with father	44	28 (63.5%)	28	9 (32%)	6.79	—	1	<.01
5. "Good" relationship with both parents—themselves harmoniously married	44	22 (50%)	28	5 (18%)	6.23	Y	1	<.01
6. Patient a member of a large sibling group numbering four to twelve	44	22 (50%)	28	7 (25%)	4.45 (By method of comparison of two variables)	—	1	<.05
7. Presence of neurotic traits in childhood	44	12 (27.5%)	28	17 (60.5%)	7.95	—	1	<.01
8. Childhood recalled as "happy"	44	35 (79.5%)	28	12 (43%)	12.09	—	2	<.02
9. Robust health in childhood	44	41 (93%)	28	19 (68%)	6.18	Y	1	<.01
10. Significant parental illness during patient's childhood	44	4 (9%)	28	14 (50%)	12.67	Y	1	<.05
11. Sociable personality	44	38 (86%)	28	12 (43%)	13.28	Y	1	<.02
12. Marital harmony in those married	36	31 (86%)	19	8 (42%)	9.64	Y	1	<.05

tions were significantly more common in the athletic group, viz. general somatic symptoms of hypochondriacal type ($P < .01$) and panic attacks ($P < .003$), but the pattern of symptoms was not sufficiently constant to justify any attempt to establish a new syndrome. Nevertheless, the existence of two quite distinct aetiological patterns emerged in these male neurotics.

(C) *Premorbid personality and life experience*

(1) *Comparison of athletic and non-athletic male neurotics*

II. 16. The conspicuous characteristic of the life history of male neurotics of *athletic* personality was the relative absence of neurotic markers. The great majority had enjoyed satisfactory personal relationships, and there was a minimal incidence of psychiatric and *physical* morbidity within the large childhood family. As a group these patients were highly extroverted and sociable and had usually enjoyed excellent health all their lives.

II. 17. By contrast, in the *non-athletic group,* neurotic markers were common, interpersonal relationships had been poor, their histories revealed much minor psychiatric morbidity in the family, major *physical* morbidity in the parents during childhood (in characteristically smaller sibling groups), and a much greater number had themselves experienced serious *physical* ill-health during childhood. They were relatively introverted and unsociable.

II. 18. These further significant differences between the two groups are shown in Table 4.

(2) *Comparison of male neurotics and matched controls*

II. 19. (a) *The athletic neurotic group differed from the controls* only with respect to their athletic zeal (v. s.) and in the greater number who showed the higher degrees of sociability (Table 5).

A product-moment correlation of $+.79$ was found between independent observers' assessments on a five point scale of the personality variable "sociability."

Table 5. Sociability

	N	Grades +2, +1 (More sociable)	Grades 0, −1, −2 (Less sociable)	Total
Athletic neurotics (male)	44	38 (86.5%)	6 (13.5%)	44 (100%)
Normal (control) males matched for age	33	15 (45%)	18 (55%)	33 (100%)

χ^2 (Yates correction) = 12.8. 1 df. $p < 0.001$.

II. 20. (b) The personalities of the *non-athletic group, however, when compared with the controls,* showed characteristics which conform more to our accepted model of the neurotically vulnerable subject. A greater number had: a family history of mild psychiatric disorder ($P < .03$), impaired relationship with mother ($P < .01$), and father ($P < .01$) during childhood, and, if married, with wife ($P < .01$), neurotic traits in childhood ($P < .01$), unhappy childhood ($P < .02$) and seriously impaired parental health during the patients' childhood ($P < .01$). A larger number had been members of a smaller sibling group of three and under during childhood ($P < .01$).

II. 21. *Age Effect:* None of the differences demonstrated between the three groups—athletic neurotics, non-athletic neurotics, and controls—can be attributed to age differences.

. . .

III. Incidence of the Athlete's Neurosis

III. 1. The following figures offer a rough guide and are based on all 387 new psychiatric cases referred to me during 1964. An exclusive diagnosis of "neurotic syndrome" was made in 22 percent of the 149 males. Approximately 40 percent of these neuroses occurred in subjects of athletic personality. Thus one in eleven (9 percent) of new male referrals seen by me over the year was suffering from the athlete's neurosis, a figure close to those for new cases of endogenous depression (13 percent) and schizophrenia (11 percent) in males.

IV. Discussion

Social influences

IV. 1. The athlete's neurosis, which is no rare, trivial or short-lived reaction, can, and usually does, provoke prolonged and crippling psychological, domestic and economic strains, as many of these men despite previous sound work records subsequently remained unemployable for years. Is this athlete's neurosis yet another disorder contingent on lowered morbidity and mortality levels associated with medical progress and relative affluence when the experience of ill-health can come as a surprise for which the individual may be ill-prepared? The condition is essentially another example of what Hill has called a "deprivation neurosis" in which conflict appears to play little part. It is a bereavement reaction to loss of part of oneself necessitating, as Lindemann has said "reorganisations which do not belong to the arsenal of habitual adjustive responses." Thus there are at least three parameters to be considered in assessing a stress-provoking experience:

intensity, duration, and relevance to the particular individual's personality and life experience, plus a possible fourth — the surprise effect of the trauma.

IV. 2. Will more men, in advanced societies, fall into the athlete's trap in the future? Perhaps the trend will be as Michael Young predicts in his provocative book *The Rise of the Meritocracy* in which, retrospecting as from the year 2033, he sees the rise of the new intellectual aristocracy following increasing equality of opportunity and promotion by merit resulting in the striving for prestige through non-intellectual alternatives, among which athleticism increasingly becomes the pabulum of the masses. "The lower classes needed a mythos," he writes, "and they got what they needed, the mythos of muscularity . . . they esteemed physical achievement almost as highly as we of the upper class esteem mental." Furthermore, as Wallach observes of athletes "They are destroyed overnight by the concept of mortality . . . these fellows are always and forever twenty-one."

Is athleticism neurotic?

IV. 3. The findings of this enquiry present a challenge to Schneider's dictum "there are no neuroses, only neurotics" and to the viewpoint advocated by Sullivan . . . "that the essence of mental illness lies in a disturbance of interpersonal relationships and that acute illness arises out of a crisis in such relationships." All the evidence in the present study points to exceptionally favourable intra- and extra- family personal relationships in the athletic group.

IV. 4. Furthermore, in this group acute illness does not arise out of a crisis in such relationships, but primarily out of the shock of a threat to overvalued but waning physical prowess. Any disturbance of interpersonal relationship present must be of a very subtle order.

IV. 5. One might well enquire why these subjects became, and remained, so fanatically and exclusively devoted to physical prowess. No one can indefinitely enjoy absolutely ideal interpersonal relationships, and no doubt ever deeper probing might well have revealed some defects in these subjects, but would they be sufficient and would they be relevant? Here surely is an occasion for the application of Occam's razor. One may accept the theory of Lorenz and conceptualise athleticism as a manifestation of the diversion of instinctual aggression into ritualised socially innocuous channels. Whatever its source I would maintain that even excessive athleticism is not in itself 'neurotic' for this premorbid behaviour is associated neither with suffering in the subject, nor in those with whom he associates. But I would concede that, like exclusive and excessive emotional dependence on work, on key family relationship-bonds, intellectual pursuits, physical beauty, sexual prowess or any other overvalued attribute or activity, athleticism can place the subject in a vulnerable pre-neurotic state leading to manifest neurotic illness in the event of an *appropriate* threat, or actual enforced deprivation, especially if abrupt or unexpected. The genesis of potentially psychopathological over-valuations does not *invariably* lie in disturbed interpersonal relationships.

V. Summary and Conclusion

V. 1. The clinical study here reported reveals a not uncommon psychological aetiology associated with the sudden development of neurotic symptoms in males of apparently robust premorbid personality. This aetiology has not previously been fully reported and is characterized by a striking absence of disturbed interpersonal relations.

V. 2. Although the concept of "neurosis" or "neurotic syndrome" has been fairly narrowly restricted in this study so as to admit only one in five of all male referrals, nevertheless, it has been demonstrated that neurotic maladjustment of acute onset occurs as a manifestation of a deprivation crisis, in the absence of evidence of early or late disturbed interpersonal relations in 40 percent of such male neurotic subjects, and that the impact of the apparently trivial but highly specific traumatic experience initiating crippling maladjustment in this group can only be understood in relation to the individual's personality and life experiences.

Student Radicalism

Of late, adults' concern with student radicalism has eclipsed their concern with juvenile delinquency. The two phenomena resemble each other to the extent that the immediate actors are youthful and their acts frequently violate laws and/or disturb order. At the same time, most juvenile delinquents come from poor families, are meagerly educated, are average or below average in intelligence, and act for the sake of immediate material gain or for no avowed reasons, whereas most student radicals come from upper-status families, are enrolled in select colleges and universities, and give suprapersonal, idealistic, political reasons for their activities.

Exercise 22. Sanity, Intellect, and Political Orientation

The intensity of controversy in the literature on student radicalism dwarfs the intensity of controversy in the literature on juvenile delinquency. Various investigators espouse competing versions of causes and cures of juvenile delinquency. But they share the belief that the phenomenon under study is deplorable. This sort of belief does not unite investigators of student radicalism. Studies of student radicalism have visibly been shaped not only by prejudices in favor of one or another general theory of social causation but also by feelings of intense sympathy or (less commonly, at present) intense hostility to the phenomenon studied. The following selection is a case in point.

Your assignment, in this case, is twofold: to answer a short quiz and then to write a general critique. The quiz questions follow the reading, as do suggestions for the critique.

Christian Bay

*Political and Apolitical Students:
Facts in Search of Theory**

I. Introduction

I. 1. Why do students active in protest movements tend to do better academically, and be more intelligent and intellectually disposed, compared to more apolitical students? There is a wealth of data to show that this is so, but an astounding absence of efforts to make theoretical sense of it. Moreover, for decades we have known that more liberal or radical students have, statistically speaking, been more intelligent or academically able than more conservative students; and similar relationships have been found with a corresponding regularity in studies, though fewer in number, of adult populations. How can we account for this apparent preponderance of intelligence and intellectual resources on the left side of the political spectrum?

I. 2. In this paper I hope to contribute toward such a theoretical accounting. My main task is to try to make theoretical sense of three categories of data, to be briefly discussed or summarized in the following sections: (a) traditional attitude measurement studies, from the 1920's on, mainly administered to students but at other times to adults, which almost invariably have found those who are more liberal doing better on intelligence, educational achievement, etc. compared to those who are more conservative; (b) work on authoritarianism and related neurotic tendencies, which again has demonstrated a clear affinity between these tendencies and rightwing views, compared to a much less clear, or more tenuous, affinity with leftwing orientations; and (c) recent work on student political activists, which abundantly shows liberal and leftist militancy to correlate with high academic or intellectual achievement.

I. 3. The attempted theoretical explanation is based on fairly recent work by social psychologists, whose theory of the functions of attitudes will be extended toward a theory of individual political rationality as an aspect of human development.

II. Traditional Studies of Radical Versus Conservative Attitudes

II. 1. The invention and subsequently the continued improvement of techniques for the measurement of attitudes, together with increasingly sophisticated techniques of correlational analysis and the related knacks of applied statistics, have stimulated an enormous number of studies of attitudes and relationships

*Reprinted by permission from *The Journal of Social Issues,* vol. 23, no. 3, 1967, pp. 76–91. An acknowledgments footnote has been deleted. The roman numerals have been added.

between attitudes, beginning around 1920. A large category of attitude studies dealt with political orientations. Among the latter studies there must have been hundreds reported in the journals of the twenties and thirties which either focussed on or paid attention to characteristics of *radical* versus *conservative* attitudes and their respective correlates.

II. 2.   There is one difference in particular between students (the major population studied) with more radical or liberal and students with more conservative views that shows up in study after study: more radical students kept scoring higher either on intelligence tests or by way of academic grades, compared to more conservative students. There were exceptions, but there is no gainsaying the general tendency. Speaking of the literature reporting research on conservative attitudes on American campuses, Newcomb reports an almost unanimous finding:

> Whatever the context of the term "conservatism," those who show it least on any given campus tend to make higher scores on intelligence tests, or to make better scholastic records, or both, than those who show it most (Newcomb, 1943, 171).

II. 3.   Beginning around 1930, there also have been a good number of studies of attitude change, especially during the college years, and more are being published today. In Newcomb's classic study of Bennington students during the late thirties, published in 1943, the fact that most students left college considerably more liberal or radical than they had been as entering freshmen is accounted for mainly in terms of peer group influence:

> ... nonconservative attitudes are developed at Bennington primarily by those who are both capable and desirous of cordial relations with their fellow community members (Newcomb, 1943, 148–149).

II. 4.   But why was Bennington a breeding ground for radicals and liberals in the 1930's? Newcomb's explanation is plausible but somewhat atheoretical: Bennington College was founded in 1932, the year FDR took office, and many faculty members were interested in and sympathetic to the New Deal, as were many other American intellectuals at the time. But is there nothing about the educational process itself that should lead us to expect, in the best colleges, a liberal rather than a conservative climate? To this question, Newcomb's otherwise excellent study does not address itself.

II. 5.   Samuel A. Stouffer, in his valuable 1955 volume, *Communism, Conformity, and Civil Liberties,* finds that community leaders invariably are more tolerant of the freedom of dissent, compared to the bulk of the population. For example, 84% of the leaders would allow a socialist to speak compared to 58% of the general population. For the atheist's right to speak, the corresponding figures are 64 compared to 37; for the communist's, 51 compared to 27. And so on.

II. 6.   Based on composites of replies to all his tolerance questions, Stouffer constructed a scale of tolerance of nonconformists. Stouffer's "more tolerant" respondents, as of May–July, 1954, are younger: 47% of those in their twenties, compared to 18% in their sixties, are "more tolerant" — and there is a linear relationship for the in-between age groups. Secondly, the more liberal respondents are better educated: 66% of the college graduates, compared to 16% of those with grade schools only, and again a clear linear relationship. Further breakdowns indicated, too, that the better educated are more liberal also for matching age levels, while the younger are more liberal also at matching levels of education. Stouffer also found that optimism concerning one's personal future — generally higher for younger than for older people — correlates highly with liberalism (or, in his terms, tolerance).

II. 7. In addition, Stouffer found a clear relationship between urbanization and liberalism, both nationally and for each region of the United States: West, East, Middle West, South. The degree of liberalism is also related to the region, with descending degrees from West to South in the order listed.

II. 8. By way of explanation of these and related findings, Stouffer suggests that a factor essential to tolerance may be "contact with people with disturbing and unpopular ideas . . . (schooling) *puts a person in touch with people whose ideas and values are different from one's own"* (1955, 125–128). Urban living does this and so, probably, does living in the West, where a higher proportion of the population has lived in other regions. The cities of the Far West "which have grown at such an astonishing rate by recruiting from all parts of this country, are the highest of all in our scale of tolerance," Stouffer has found (1955, 127–128).

II. 9. But why is it that the younger people, regardless of levels of education, tend to be more liberal than the older people? The only hypothesis Stouffer suggests is that it is easier for the young to be optimistic about their personal future; and degrees of optimism ("my life will be better") are significantly related to youth and also to tolerance, as his data bear out. But why should optimists tend to be tolerant of nonconformists? Stouffer here merely states that "there is substantial psychological theory which would predict a relationship between optimism about personal affairs and tolerance toward nonconformists"; he elaborates only to the extent of suggesting the need for scapegoats for individuals who are very troubled and the availability of communists and other nonconformists as "obvious targets for blame, directly for the world's troubles and indirectly, if sometimes unconsciously, for one's personal troubles" (Stouffer, 1955, 100). Is this all there is to the relationship he demonstrated between youth and liberalism?

III. Personality and Political Attitudes

III. 1. In *The Authoritarian Personality* a number of factors were found to be related to neurotic authoritarianism as measured by the F-scale. Among these were political-economic conservatism, measured by the PEC scale in its several forms, all of which gave a high score to respondents indicating a high degree of "support of the *status quo* and particularly of business; support of conservative values; desire to maintain a balance of power in which business is dominant, labor subordinate and the economic functions of government minimized; and resistance to social change" (Adorno, et al., 1950, 154–155).

Rokeach's criticisms

III. 2. There are serious methodological shortcomings in this work, as is often the case with pioneering ventures. While Edward Shils had charged the authors of *The Authoritarian Personality* with a kind of ideological blindness to the phenomenon of authoritarianism on the Left, a charge based on political assumptions of his own rather than substantive evidence (Bay, 1965, 209–10), Milton Rokeach, one of the work's major critics, has made a more specific charge. He has stated that there was something wrong with the F-scale; it was politically slanted and could tap only rightwing-dogmatism (Rokeach, 1956, 1960). To demonstrate that he could remedy this defect, Rokeach developed not only a Dogmatism scale which claimed to be politically neutral along major conventional right–left dimensions; he also proceeded to substantiate this claim by developing two Opinionation scales, one measuring vehement intolerance of leftist views and the other doing the same for rightist views. Having achieved a reasonably high reliability for both Opinionation scales in several samples, Rokeach proceeded to demonstrate that his Dogmatism scale, *unlike* the F-scale, the E-scale and the PEC scale, correlated positively not only with his Right Opinionation scale but with his Left Opinionation scale as well.

III. 3. Strictly speaking there probably is no such thing as a politically neutral scale, unless it be devoid of all social content; what Rokeach showed is that the F-scale does not, while his own Dogmatism scale does correlate with the degrees of vehemence (which presumably were symptomatic of the closedmindedness) with which leftist as well as rightist opinions are held, at least in certain populations. As a matter of fact, Rokeach notes that both his Dogmatism scale and his combined Opinionation scale show a weak but consistently positive relationship to conservatism, and also that Dogmatism in all his samples shows somewhat closer affinity to Right than to Left Opinionation. He raises but dismisses perhaps too lightly the possibility that his scales are less neutral than intended; his principal explanation is that communism, unlike fascism, is humanitarian in its ideology (or *content,* as he puts it), at least; and that the same, to a more modest extent, may be true of liberal versus conservative ideology. In support of his belief that the psychological functions of communist beliefs may differ from those of fascist beliefs he cites the phenomenon of *disillusionment* which, he believes, occurs far more often among former communists than among former nazis or fascists, indicating a sudden awareness of contradictions within the communist creed which may not exist within fascist creeds, whose, anti-humanism pertains to ends as well as means, or content as well as structure. He also refers to Robert Lindner's theory that communists more often have neurotic problems, often guilt-related, while fascists more often are psychopaths, or people with an underdeveloped conscience (Lindner, 1953).

McClosky's findings

III. 4. Another, more massive study comparing conservatives to liberals is reported by Herbert McClosky, whose more than 2000 respondents were drawn from Minnesota population samples. These are his principal findings of relevance here: (a) "By every measure available to us, conservative beliefs are found most frequently among the uninformed, the poorly educated and so far as we can determine, the less intelligent"; (b) "Conservatism, in our society at least, appears to be far more characteristic of social isolates, of people who think poorly of themselves . . . who are submissive, timid, and wanting in confidence"; and (c) "In the four liberal-conservative classifications, the extreme conservatives are easily the most hostile and suspicious, the most rigid and compulsive, the quickest to condemn others for their imperfections and weaknesses, the most intolerant, the most inflexible and unyielding in their perceptions and judgments. Although aggressively critical of the shortcomings of others, they are unusually defensive and armored in the protection of their own ego needs. Poorly integrated psychologically, anxious, often perceiving themselves as inadequate, and subject to excessive feelings of guilt, they seem inclined to project onto others the traits they most dislike in themselves" (McClosky, 1958, 35–38).

III. 5. McClosky divided his respondents into four categories: "liberals," "moderate liberals," "moderate conservatives" and "extreme conservatives"; these labels suggest that he felt he had more "extreme" conservatives than liberals in his main samples. The three tables he presented are astoundingly consistent in yielding entirely linear correlations from "liberal" to "extreme conservative," without a single exception; "moderate liberals," for example, are found to be higher on hostility, lower on education and intellectuality, etc., than "liberals"; and McClosky claims that his data "could be buttressed by numerous other related findings" (1958, 38).

III. 6. McClosky's analysis of these striking findings is couched more in descriptive than in developmental terms. For example: "From whatever direction we approach him, the prototypic conservative seems far more impelled to contain, to reject, and to take precautions against, his fellow creatures" (1958, 38). But why? McClosky is cautious indeed on this score. The closest thing to a suggestion of a causal relationship is his statement that "education is likely to lead to liberal rather than conservative tendencies" (1958, 41). Among his concluding cautionary remarks, he says that conservative doctrines "appear, in some measure, to arise from personality needs, but it is conceivable at least, that both are the product of some third set of factors." Conservatism and a host of undesirable personality traits clearly, in these Minnesota samples, "go together. *How* they go together, and which is antecedent to which, is a more difficult and more elusive problem" (1958, 44).

III. 7. There has been a remarkable lack of follow-up of this striking demonstration of affinity between degrees of conservatism and widely disvalued personality and social characteristics. If *The Authoritarian Personality's* findings of affinity between conservatism and neurotic authoritarianism can be questioned on methodological grounds, and if Rokeach's data only mildly suggested a similar affinity, McClosky's tables appear methodologically solid and of great theoretical import.

IV. Recent Work on Student Activists

IV. 1. I shall not attempt an exhaustive survey of all available data on student activism or student leftism generally. The reader is referred to several of the articles in this issue for a summary of these data; the articles by Trent and Craise and by Flacks are particularly relevant. Of especial importance to the line of argument which I have been developing are the following findings.

Berkeley, 1957 — Selvin and Hagstrom findings

IV. 2. Hanan C. Selvin and Warren O. Hagstrom in December, 1957, while things were still fairly quiet on the Berkeley campus, did a study of the views on civil liberties in a sample of 894 Berkeley students (Selvin and Hagstrom, 1965). Anticipating that abstract statements favoring the Bill of Rights would sooner indicate conformism than liberalism, these investigators elicited responses to specific civil liberties issues involving conflicts with other values. On the basis of these responses they constructed a Libertarianism Index. They divided their sample into three groups: highly libertarian (34%), moderately libertarian (46%), slightly libertarian (20%).

IV. 3. Of interest here are the data comparing the highly libertarian students with the Berkeley student body in general. In a linear relationship, again, the proportions of highly libertarian students on the Berkeley campus ascend from freshman to senior graduate level: 21% — 29% — 34% — 40% — 54%. The relationship between libertarianism and grades is inconclusive in the lower division but clear in the upper division: among A to B+ students 54% are "highly-libertarian," compared to 37% among B to C+ students and 25% among students at C level or below.

IV. 4. Children of blue collar workers among Berkeley students are libertarians more often, by a wide margin, than are children of parents better able to support their offspring financially through college; this is true in spite of the fact that blue collar parents average lower educational attainments than other parents and are likely to be relatively non-libertarian themselves. "Greater economic independence, in the sense of self-support," conclude Selvin and Hagstrom, "is strongly associated with having more libertarian attitudes than one's parents" (Selvin and Hagstrom, 1965, 504).

IV. 5. Among male students the social science and humanities majors were by a wide margin found more libertarian than the rest, with engineering and education (a field that has recruited low achievers in Berkeley) and business administration at the bottom. Among female students, social welfare majors were most libertarian, while life science majors shared the next level of libertarianism with social science and humanities majors, and with education majors once again at the bottom. And, finally, fraternity and especially sorority students—who are least likely to get to know well people with unorthodox ideas—are least likely to be libertarians, compared to students with other living arrangements.

Berkeley, 1964—Somers' data

IV. 6. In November, 1964, when the student rebellion at Berkeley was under way, Robert H. Somers interviewed a carefully drawn sample of 285 Berkeley students. He found 63% to favor the goals of the Free Speech Movement, while about 34% approved the FSM's tactics; clearly favoring goals as well as tactics were 30%, and Somers calls this group the *militants,* while the *moderates,* again 30%, clearly supported FSM's goals but not the means used, and 22% *conservatives* were opposed to the ends sought as well as the tactics used (Somers, 1964).

IV. 7. For my purposes the crucial findings of this study are summarized as follows by Somers: "it is hard to overlook the fact that in our sample there is a strong relation between academic achievement and support for the demonstrators. Among those who reported to our interviewers a grade point average of B+ or better, nearly half (45 percent) are militants, and only a tenth are conservatives. At the other end, over a third of those with an average of B— or less are conservatives, and only 15 percent are militants." If the FSM represented a minority of students, Somers concluded, it would be "a minority vital to the excellence of this university" (1964, 544).

Berkeley 1965—Heist's findings

IV. 8. Early in 1965 Paul Heist did a study of a sample drawn from a list of more than 800 persons said to have been arrested in the Sproul Hall sit-in (Heist, 1965). On advice of their legal counsel, about 50% of the 33% sample refused to return the questionnaire but the rest cooperated, 128 in all; an additional 60 FSM activists were recruited subsequently as subjects for the study. In addition, a random sample of 92 seniors (class of 1964–1965) were given the same two questionnaires. Also, Heist had access to the same attitude inventory data from 340 seniors (class of 1962–1963) and from "2500+" entering freshmen, all at Berkeley. Further details of this study by Heist plus other related work are presented by Trent and Craise in this issue.

IV. 9. Heist developed an Intellectual Disposition Index on the basis of six of the twelve scales in his attitude inventory, and with this instrument divided his FSM sample and his three general student samples according to eight "degrees," from low to high Intellectual Disposition. Here is what he found:

> For the total FSM ground we find almost 70 percent in the top three categories and none in the bottom three, and it is to be remembered that a large proportion, in fact, the majority, of the FSM persons were freshmen, sophomore and juniors. The number of persons in these upper categories in the senior sample amounts to 25 and 31 percent. The Free Speech Movement drew extraordinarily larger proportions of students with strong intellectual orientations, at all levels (freshmen through graduate) (Heist, 1965, 21–22a).

Watts and Whittaker and FSM

IV. 10. William A. Watts and David N. E. Whittaker's study of FSM activists compared to Berkeley students generally started with this hypothesis: "We expected that FSM members would be more flexible as defined and measured by personality tests of flexibility–rigidity . . . than their counterparts who were less committed, neutral, or even opposed to the Movement" (Watts and Whittaker, 1966, 43).

IV. 11. Their study was based on questionnaires administered to a chance sample of 172 participants among the 1000–1200 students who "sat in" at Sproul Hall in the afternoon of December 2, 1964, (and who were on this occasion not arrested, or not yet, except for the two thirds who stayed on all night). In addition, the same questionnaire was given to a random sample of 182 Berkeley students at about the same time; 146 of these cooperated. The instrument included a 27-item rigidity–flexibility scale. The most important result of this study, for present purposes, is its indication of "strong support for the prediction of greater flexibility among the FSM members" (1966, 59). The authors conclude that this latter finding is of particular interest considering the purported rigidity of the FSM members in negotiations with the University administration, and suggests the necessity of distinguishing between a trait of rigidity as psychologically defined and commitment.

IV. 12. Two other findings of the study by Watts and Whittaker should be noted in passing. First, with an additional sample of 181 students drawn from the District Attorney's arrest list for December 3, and 174 names drawn at random from the Student Directory, they failed to establish greater academic achievement on the part of the FSM'ers compared to other students, and concluded that these activists were quite typical or average with respect to grade point averages (1966, 52). While Watts and Whittaker's objective check is more trustworthy than the data on grade point averages reported in the Somers study which were based on respondents' information, I am inclined to discount, until substantiated by further research, this particular finding by Watts and Whittaker, because it appears to run counter to so many other findings discussed in this article. It may well be valid for the 773 who were arrested, though I would have liked to see a replication of the study, which can easily be done; if it is valid for this group, I would still doubt that it is valid for FSM activists generally. It is possible, for example, that the most *academically* as distinct from *intellectually* oriented students among FSM activists felt greater anxiety than the rest about their academic credits, and were more likely to shrink from taking the most extreme risks.

IV. 13. Secondly, the FSM students were far more likely to have parents with advanced academic degrees, compared to the cross-section sample: "approximately 26 percent of the fathers and 16 percent of the mothers of the FSM sample possess either Ph.D. or M.A. degrees compared to 11 percent and 4 percent respectively in the cross-section" (Watts and Whittaker, 1966, 53 and Table 4). This finding does not contradict Somers' finding that student militants were more likely than the rest to have blue-collar fathers. Among several factors that could be taken into account here, I would emphasize the difference between having militant attitudes and being prepared to jeopardize academic achievements; the value of academic credits may well loom somewhat larger to the self-supporting student from a working class background, than they do to students from families in which academic proficiency or intellectual gifts or future financial safety tends to be taken for granted. The latter category among the militants may be more likely to risk jail and expulsion for their beliefs.

IV. 14. I have confined this brief inquiry to activists on the Left, who are far more significant than those on the Right, both by their numbers (at least in the better universities), and by their tendency to persist in political activities disturbing to the university "image" desired by most administrators and trustees. In so far as rightist student groups, the most important one among them at the moment being Young Americans for Freedom, have staged demonstrations, they have usually been *ad hoc* counter-demonstrations, directed *against* issue-oriented protests by liberal or leftist student activists; there have been no protracted campaigning or even articulate political programs; and while student leftists have tended to be fiercely independent of older leftists, or of the "generation over thirty" generally, there has been no evidence of a corresponding intellectual independence among organized rightist students.

V. Toward a Psychological Theory of Radical Versus Conservative Attitudes

V. 1. The most promising approach to theorizing about the psychological nature of liberal and radical *versus* conservative political attitudes, I believe, is to consider what kind of functions political opinions may serve for those who hold them, in terms of their personality and social needs. It is quickly apparent that the function of serving a rational, realistic understanding of the political world is one but only one possible function of a person's "politics."

*Types of motives underlying
political opinions*

V. 2. The over-all function of any political or other social opinion, write M. Brewster Smith, Jerome S. Bruner and Robert W. White, (1960, 275) is to strike a "compromise between reality demands, social demands, and inner psychological demands." Daniel Katz (1960) distinguishes between rationality (or reality-testing) motives, value-expressive motives, social acceptance motives, and ego defense motives. These are suggested analytical categories; specific opinions usually serve a mixture of needs or motives. The relative weight of each type of motive varies from person to person, from attitude to attitude and from time to time; few of us, if any, are free of neurotic ego defensiveness, and none of us are free of social acceptance needs or desires for consistency and for realistic understanding of the world in which we live.

V. 3. In their 1954 paper, Irving Sarnoff and Daniel Katz applied their three categories of motives in a discussion of a clearly *undesirable* type of attitude, namely anti-Negro prejudice; and one of their main concerns was to show how a better understanding of the motives of attitudes could facilitate processes of attitude change. Thus, to the extent that prejudice is rationally founded — on the basis, say, of the limited knowledge available to many a Southern American white boy or girl, it presumably can be influenced by new knowledge. To the extent, however, that prejudice is based on social acceptance motives, it will take evidence that such a change of opinion would not reduce a person's acceptance in whatever groups he wants to be or become part of. To the extent, finally, that ego defensive motives determine the prejudice, it may take psychotherapy to reduce it.

Ego defensive motives . . .

V. 4. There is evidence, wrote Gardner Murphy more than twenty years ago, "that functional intelligence can be enormously enhanced, first by the systematic study and removal of individual and socially shared autisms, second, by the cultivation of curiosity, and third, by the art of withdrawal from the pressures of immediate external tasks, to let the mind work at its own pace and in its own congenial way" (Murphy, 1945, 16).

V. 15. The most fundamental obstacle, of course, to the "freeing of intelligence" is the active presence of ego defensive motives. Severely repressed anxieties about one's worth as a human being, which may well be the result of a childhood starved of affection, may predestine a person to become a "true believer" in Eric Hoffer's sense — a person who seeks a new collective identity because he cannot live with his own self (Hoffer, 1951). Such anxieties, if unresolved, may predestine a person to become an authoritarian or an anti-authoritarian personality (cf. Bay, 1965, 207–217), a bigot, a rightwinger, or, more rarely, a left-winger. This type of person is not psychologically free; his views may keep his anxieties and fears manageable but contributes no realistic understanding of the external political world.

V. 6. Some of the data discussed previously can be understood in this light; Adorno et al., Rokeach and McClosky all found rightwing views statistically associated with indices of neurosis of one kind or another. But what of McClosky's finding that, for example, "liberals" appeared less hostile than "moderate liberals," and what of the data on student activists?

Social acceptance motives . . .

V. 7. To account for such data we need to consider the prevalence of social acceptance motives, too, as obstacles to the freeing of political intelligence. To the extent that a person is deeply worried about his popularity, his career prospects, his financial future, his reputation, etc., he will utilize his political opinions not for achieving realistic insight but for impressing his reference groups and his reference persons favorably. These processes of obfuscation may be conscious or, more likely, subconscious, but they are above all pervasive in our society, and in every other society, too—above all in highly competitive and socially mobile societies, in which the difference between "success" and lack of it may make for vast differences in prospects for the satisfaction of physical and self-esteem needs, and perhaps for many other kinds of needs as well. Social acceptance-motivated political beliefs serve the individual's desired image, status and career, etc., but contribute little toward a realistic understanding of his political world—at least in so far as it extends beyond his immediate reference groups and persons.

V. 8. Social acceptance-motivated opinions may well tend to be liberal in some university faculties, as charged by some conservative writers, including conservative students wishing to explain why liberalism increases with amount of education (cf. Naylor, 1966 for a discussion of this). But by and large, in every stable social order, they tend to be conservative, or at most mildly liberal, firmly within the established framework of constitutional objectives and processes. In every stable society there are rich and poor, strong and weak, privileged and underprivileged; and not only political power and influence but social status and respectability are associated with seeing political problems through the eyes of the former rather than the latter, in each paired category.

V. 9. Statistically speaking, therefore, *more conservative views, among students or adults generally, are likely to be less rationally, less independently motivated, compared to more radical-liberal views.*

V. 10. I am by no means arguing, of course, that liberal and radical views cannot be neurotically motivated. The point is a more modest one; the frequency of neurotic motivations—now including not only deeply repressed anxieties about the individual's own worth but also milder ego deficiencies such as constant worry about popularity or career prospects—is probably higher the further away the politically active person is from the left side of the political spectrum (I did not say left *end*).

V. II. The statistical data surveyed make good sense if viewed in this perspective. With reference to the Berkeley data, surely one should expect ego defensiveness to be manifested by a fear of anarchy and equality, and lead the individual to detest both the style and the objectives of FSM-type movements. And the more intensely or neurotically one is preoccupied with career worries, the less one would be disposed to mingle with the student rebels; these students, more typically, appear to have decided that certain values are more dear to them than conventional career prospects. The articles by [Kenneth] Keniston and [Richard] Flacks made this same point. As rebels they are more likely to have made a choice and to have marshalled the intellectual and emotional resources, at some point, to stick to it, also in situations of severe stress. Obviously, some will for spurious or chance reasons pursue neurotic social acceptance needs with FSM-type groups as their reference systems; but this happens in almost every group, and is likely to occur with less frequency in a rebellious political action group than in less demanding and socially more homogeneous groups like, for example, fraternities and sororities.

"Only rebellion can expand consciousness"

V. 12. As Albert Camus saw, only rebellion, on some level, can expand consciousness; "with rebellion, awareness is born." Awareness of being human — of being more than an aspiring carpenter, merchant, lawyer, educator or military officer. Or dutiful son or daughter.

> In our daily trials rebellion plays the same role as does the "cogito" in the realm of thought: it is the first piece of evidence. But this evidence lures the individual from his solitude. It founds its first value on the whole human race. I rebel — therefore we exist (Camus, 1958, 15 and 22).

V. 13. Camus' portrait of the rebel presents a normative ideal in persuasive terms: to become fully human, a constant tendency to be revolted by and to rebel against oppression and injustice is required. While I admit to sharing this normative position, my present argument is empirical, though speculative: I submit that it will help make sense of all the data reviewed in this paper if we consider Camus' rebel a developmental model — a *probable* type of person to develop *to the extent that* not only ego defensive but more mildly neurotic social acceptance anxieties are resolved or successfully faced up to.

V. 14. This kind of theory is bound to be speculative if only because such social anxieties are so pervasive. Yet it is possible to argue that the various data associating leftism with academic competence, intelligence, psychological and socio-economic security, etc., may be seen as tending to support this theory. Further research in this area is desirable and feasible, and can be usefully focused by this kind of theory.[1]

V. 15. The more secure and sheltered a person's infancy and childhood, and the more freedom that educational and other social processes has given him to develop according to his inner needs and potentialities, the more likely that a capacity for political rationality and independence will develop, simply because the likelihood of severe anxieties is relatively low. In addition, again converting Camus' ideal into empirical-theoretical currency, the better the individual has been able to resolve his own anxieties, the more likely that he will empathize with others less fortunate than himself. A sense of justice as well as a capacity for rationality is, according to this theory, a likely development in relatively secure individuals, whose politics, if any, will therefore tend toward the left—toward supporting the champions of the underdog, not the defenders of established, always unjust, institutions. And young people, with the proverbial impetuousness of youth, are likely to seek extremes of social justice, or militant means, simply because their emotions, and more particularly their sense of elementary morality and justice, have not yet been dulled by daily compromises and defeats to the extent that most older persons' emotions have been.[2]

---

[1] One Polish study by Hannah E. Malewska, for example, ought to be followed up: she found that children's notions of moral norms become more responsible (less formal and superficial) the less severely disciplinarian their parents and the more urbanized their surroundings (Malewska, 1961). Work on children's politics is on the increase, but often restricts itself unduly to cognitive aspects. An exception is the work of Fred J. Greenstein (1965).

Patricia Richmond and I a few years ago found that among liberals in a pacifistically oriented organization, the more "extreme" supporters of rights of specific unpopular minorities tended to be somewhat less dogmatic in Rokeach's sense, than the more moderate supporters of such rights (Bay and Richmond, 1960). More work is needed to improve on instruments like Rokeach's Dogmatism scale, and to develop additional instruments to measure neurotic obstacles to rationality in the general population, so that we might discover how widely and in what types of contexts it is true that resolution of anxieties and reduction of other psychological burdens stimulate tendencies toward rationality, political activism, leftism and related phenomena.

Let me in conclusion mention the valuable, still small but apparently growing literature that seeks in-depth understanding of the political views and their motivations in particular individuals, whether prominent or humble, and whether dead or still living. A masterly political biographical study in psychological terms is *Woodrow Wilson and Colonel House* by Alexander and Juliette George (1956). Justly famous is Erik H. Erikson's *Young Man Luther* (1958). Arnold A. Rogow's *James T. Forrestal* is particularly valuable for its searching analysis of the issues associated with possible mental disorder in high office (1964). Among psychological studies of the politics of humbler individuals, who are left anonymous, reference has been made to *Opinions and Personality* by M. Brewster Smith et al. (1960), a study limiting its scope to attitudes toward the Soviet Union. Three other very useful works are Robert E. Lane's *Political Ideology*, a study of fifteen "average" New Englanders, mostly working men; David Riesman's *Faces in the Crowd,* dealing with "average" Los Angelese; and an excellent Australian study of five more or less politically active individuals—*Private Politics* by Alan F. Davies (1966).

[2] Now there are some older persons, too, who for all the toll of many years of practical experience, seem to have remained able to share the basic moral and political outlook (if not necessarily the views on tactics) of militant student activists. As I read some of Erik H. Erikson's recent work, he appears to conclude that man's sense of social responsibility and his degree of social sensitivity depend on his

V. 16. Let me sharpen my own position as follows: *Every new human being is potentially a liberal animal and a rebel; yet every social organization he will be up against, from the family to the state, is likely to seek to "socialize" him into a conveniently pliant conformist.*

V. 17. Many parents and some schools are child-oriented to the extent of trying to give children the security and freedom to develop according to their own inner needs and potentialities. With a good start of this kind, such children may, when they approach adulthood, be able to resist the socializing of privilege-defending states, universities and other established institutional pillars of the *status quo;* if so, they become the student rebels, the civil rights workers, and the peace activists: a small minority, but a growing one in terms of influence among young people.

References

Adorno, Theodore W., Frenkel-Brunswik, E., Levinson, D. J. and Sanford, R. N. *The authoritarian personality.* New York: Harper, 1950.

Bay, Christian. *Structure of freedom.* New York: Atheneum, 1965 (1958).

Bay, Christian and Richmond, Patricia. Some varieties of Liberal experience. Unpublished paper, 1960.

Camus, Albert. *The rebel.* New York: Vintage, 1958.

Davies, Alan F. *Private politics.* Melbourne: Melbourne University Press, 1966.

Erikson, Erik H. *Young man Luther.* New York: Norton, 1958.

Erikson, Erik H. *Insight and responsibility.* New York: Norton, 1964.

George, Alexander and George, Juliette. *Woodrow Wilson and Colonel House.* New York: John Day, 1956.

Greenstein, Fred J. *Children and politics.* New Haven: Yale University Press, 1965.

Heist, Paul. Intellect and commitment: The faces of discontent. Center for the Study of Higher Education, Berkeley, 1965. (mimeo)

Hoffer, Eric. *The true believer.* New York: Harper, 1951.

Katz, Daniel. The functional approach to the study of attitudes. *Public Opinion Quarterly,* **24,** 1960, 163–204.

Lane, Robert E. *Political ideology.* New York: Free Press, 1962.

Lindner, Robert. Political creed and character. *Psychoanalysis,* **2,** 1953, 10–33.

Malewska, Hannah E. Religious ritualism, rigid ethics, and severity in upbringing. *Polish Sociological Bulletin,* **1,** 1961, 71–78.

---

maturation beyond the Freudian psychosocial stage of genitality; he calls this hypothetically higher developmental stage *generativity:* "I refer to man's *love for his works and ideas as well as for his children,* and the necessary self-verification which adult man's ego receives, and must receive, from his labor's challenge. As adult man needs to be needed, so — for the strength of his ego and for that of his community — he requires the challenge emanating from what he has generated and from what now must be "brought up," guarded, preserved — and eventually transcended" (Erikson, 1964, 130–132). Erikson describes parenthood as "the first, and for many, the prime generative encounter" but argues that those who approach or reach the generative stage of psychosocial development to that extent *need* to teach, to instruct and influence, and in other ways actively work for the good of not only their own children but of their community and their society, or mankind, as well.

McClosky, Herbert. Conservatism and personality. *American Political Science Review,* **52,** 1958, 27–45.

Murphy, Gardner. The freeing of intelligence. *Psychological Bulletin,* **42,** 1945, 1–19.

Naylor, Robert W. Why intellectuals are liberal. *Western Politica,* **1,** 1966, 33–37.

Newcomb, Theodore M. *Personality and social change.* New York: Holt, Rinehart and Winston, 1943.

Riesman, David. *Faces in the crowd.* New York: Free Press, 1952.

Rogow, Arnold A. *James T. Forrestal.* New York: Macmillan, 1964.

Rokeach, Milton. Political and religious dogmatism: An alternative to the authoritarian personality. *Psychological Monographs,* **70,** 1956, 1–43.

Rokeach, Milton. *The open and closed mind.* New York: Basic Books, 1960.

Sarnoff, Irving and Katz, Daniel. The motivational bases of attitude change. *Journal of Abnormal and Social Psychology,* 49, 1954, 115–124.

Selvin, Hanan C. and Hagstrom, Warren O. Determinants of support for civil liberties. In Seymour M. Lipset and Sheldon S. Wolin (Eds.), *The Berkeley student revolt.* New York: Anchor, 1965, 494–518.

Shils, Edward. Authoritarianism: Right and Left. In Richard Christie and Marie Jahoda (Eds.), *Studies in the scope and method of "The authoritarian personality."* New York: Free Press, 1954.

Smith, M. Brewster, Bruner, Jerome S. and White, Robert W. *Opinions and personality.* New York: Wiley, 1960.

Somers, Robert H. The mainsprings of the rebellion: A survey of Berkeley students in November, 1964. In Seymour M. Lipset and Sheldon S. Wolin (Eds.), *The Berkeley student revolt.* New York: Anchor, 1965, 530–557.

Stouffer, Samuel A. *Communism, conformity, and civil liberties.* New York: Wiley, 1955.

Watts, William A. and Whittaker David. Free Speech Advocates at Berkeley. *Journal of Applied Behavioral Science,* 2, 1966, 41–62.

Test I

Label each of the following statements "true" or "false," and explain your answer by reference to appropriate passages in Christian Bay's essay.

1. According to Bay, post-"traditional" studies show that Leftist activists have achieved higher grade point averages than their fellow students.

2. According to Bay, neurosis is a barrier to intelligence.

3. According to Bay, persons who are active on the left politically disclose a lower incidence of neurosis than persons at the center.

4. According to Bay, people active in such groups as the Free Speech Movement at Berkeley hold opinions of the kind studied by Stouffer (on toleration) and by Selvin and Hagstrom (on libertarianism).

5. As described by Bay, Stouffer's research is consistent with the notion that people who are "more liberal" than average also are more intelligent and less neurotic.

6. According to Bay, the probability of holding true opinions is a function of the motivations that underlie opinion selection.

Test II

Compose a critical review of Bay's essay, identifying and appraising what the author undertakes to show, how he goes about his tasks, and how successful he is.

In organizing and developing your critique, you may profit from the short-answer quiz as well as these questions: To what extent and in what way does the author establish the existence of what he undertakes to explain? What explanatory themes does he espouse? Do the studies he cites yield the results he states (as in I.2)? Do they yield results compatible with earlier (I.1) and later (V) claims about association and causation? How does he undertake to substantiate his explanation or explanations? What would he *need* to do to substantiate his explanation or explanations? To what extent, and on what occasions, does Bay compare left with right, left with non-left, and left with center? What is at stake in these different kinds of comparisons?

Political Forms: Democracy

Starting about 150 years ago, in growing numbers and with increasing conviction, men of learning came to believe that the best form of government for human beings is democracy. This belief has profoundly shaped the character of modern social science. It has inspired many investigators to specialize in identifying the conditions—physical, social, economic, legal, cultural, external—that facilitate and obstruct the establishment or the maintenance of democratic rule. Such investigations express a desire to understand whether and to what extent democracy not only is beneficial but also is practicable.

Exercise 23. Is Oligarchy Unavoidable?

One of the most famous and most disturbing elements in modern democratic theory is "the iron law of oligarchy." This ominous phrase first appeared as the title of a chapter in *Political Parties: A Sociological Study of the Oligarchical Tendencies of Modern Democracy,* published in 1911 and translated into English in 1915. The author, or discoverer, of "the iron law" was Robert Michels (1876–1936), a German-born sociologist, in early life a militant Socialist and later an Italian Fascist. Commentators in abundance have alluded to "the iron law." Although they have generally agreed that the implications of "the iron law" are adverse for democracy, they have differed in what they depict as the precise terms and the foundations of this "law." The following selection is an ostensible explication of Michels's "iron law of oligarchy."

Your assignment is to discuss the logical fit between the effect or effects and the cause or causes ascribed in this statement to Michels. These questions may prove helpful: What meaning or meanings are assigned to the term *oligarchy*?

What claims are made about the incidence, historically and/or circumstantially, of oligarchy? What forces or causes are said to produce effects associated with the term *oligarchy*?

Geraint Parry

The Iron Law of Oligarchy*

1. In the main work of [Gaetano] Mosca's disciple, Robert Michels, the ideological context is kept more firmly under control. Michels treats more methodically, in *Political Parties,* theories which Mosca had proposed but not fully developed. Once again the central theme is that elite control depends upon organization. Michels extends this to mean not merely that organizational ability grants power but that the very structure of any organized society gives rise inevitably to an elite. In Michels' celebrated formulation: "Who says organization, says oligarchy."

2. Michels' method of investigation was, perhaps, the most rigidly "scientific" of any of the "classical" elitists. He proposed a hypothetical law governing all social organizations—the celebrated "iron law of oligarchy"—and then proceeded to test the hypothesis by examining the organization which *prima facie* seemed to constitute the outstanding counter-examples to the law. The organizations studied were the socialist parties of Europe in the years before the war and in particular the German socialist party. These parties were dedicated to preserving equality and democracy in their internal organization. They regarded their leaders as mere agents of the mass party. Sovereignty within the party lay with the conference of the party composed of elected delegates. The parties devised machinery such as frequent elections, to ensure that "the party leads and the leaders follow." Leadership was constantly distrusted, particularly middle-class intellectual leadership in what were basically proletarian parties. It is, however, Michels's contention that even such organizations, devoted to the negation of any tendency towards elite control, nevertheless display the "iron law of oligarchy."

3. Michels never offered a precise formulation of the law of oligarchy but its meaning is clear. In any organization of any size leadership becomes necessary to its success and survival. The nature of organization is such that it gives power and advantages to the group of leaders who cannot then be checked or held accountable by their followers. This is true despite the fact that where the leadership is elected the leaders are supposedly the agents of those electing them. There are two sets of factors which cause this result—organizational factors and psychological. Of these the organizational factors are by far the most significant.

4. Michels argues that as soon as human co-operative activities attain the size

* Reprinted by permission of Praeger Publishers, Inc. and George Allen & Unwin Ltd. from *Political Elites,* 1969, pp. 42–45. Footnotes have been deleted.

and complexity which warrant the term "organization," technical expertise is required if the enterprise is not to founder. Like Max Weber before him, Michels insists that attempts at control of an organization by the mass of its members involves an amateurishness totally self-defeating in an age of large-scale organization. A political party campaigning to gain power needs to organize its vote, canvass supporters, supply information for speakers, raise contributions, attend to the party's financial structure and its legal standing. It needs to establish a co-ordinated policy line for the sake of consistency and solidarity. All these activities require expertise which the mass of members may not have the aptitude to develop and for which they certainly lack the leisure. Mass control conflicts with efficiency and is replaced by professional direction both in policy-making and in technical administration. The result of this "technical indispensability of leadership" is that control of the party passes into the hands of its leading politicians and its bureaucracy.

5. Michels then demonstrates that power breeds power—a central tenet of elitism. The leadership controls the party funds and the party's channels of information—notably its newspaper—it attempts to select parliamentary candidates, it dispenses patronage. Its activities are news, publicized even by the opposition press. An important feature in Michels' analysis is his recognition of the impact that the party's role in the whole political system of the society has on the internal power structure of the party. Power for the party necessitates electoral success. Electoral success, however, requires the support of voters who are not necessarily party members—people who are less committed to party principle, who are on the "margin" of the party. To gain their allegiance the party must moderate its dogma, must provide continuity of leadership to give an assurance of stability, must devote itself to organizing its vote rather than maintaining the purity of its doctrine.

6. These factors, Michels suggests, strengthen the hands of two groups. Firstly, it strengthens the expert party bureaucrats more interested in the technique of power than concerned with principle. Secondly, it strengthens the elected parliamentary representatives of the party whose election gives them added weight within the party, but who owe their electoral success to their appeal to the electorate at large rather than to the much narrower party membership. The party leaders thus owe their power within the party in large part to their support outside the party. The party members cannot readily depose the leadership without damaging the party's electoral standing.

7. Ultimately the party is forced to adopt a hierarchy which mirrors the hierarchical power structure in the political system as a whole with "shadow" ministers supported by an efficient bureaucracy. Mass control is discovered to be incompatible with political power and so oligarchy triumphs, with the leadership proven to be "stable and irremovable." Even the attempts to maintain a proletarian leadership for the proletarian parties and thus prevent the estrangement between leader and led is, Michels insists, foredoomed to failure. Instead a "proletarian elite" emerges which ceases to be proletarian in anything but origin

as it exchanges manual for desk work and wages for salary. The leaders are "bourgeoisified," strangers to their class, and the party hierarchy becomes an established career offering a rise in social status as well as income.

8. These organizational and structural forces pushing towards oligarchy are reinforced, in Michels' view, by certain psychological forces, largely of a negative kind. Whilst socialist theorists have often assumed a high degree of political interest and spontaneity on the part of the bulk of the population, Michels alleges that the majority is apathetic towards public matters. Most people are only concerned with politics when it affects their private interests. They have no knowledge of how the political system works. The same applies to the members of party organizations. There is a small inner group who constitute the party *active* and are the truly influential. Below this group activity, interest and influence in the party may be represented by a pyramid—voluntary party officials, a larger stratum of those regularly attending meetings, a larger stratum still of enrolled members and, finally, a large basis of non-members who merely vote for the party.

9. For Michels, apathy goes with technical incompetence in political matters. Political knowledge has to be organized to be effective and in Michels' description the majority is too apathetic to organize itself. Such men have, he believes, a psychological need for guidance. They are glad to have others take on political responsibilities. Even revolutionary agitation has to be undertaken by a small minority on their behalf. Such apathy, submissiveness and deference provide ideal conditions for the few with the interest and the organizational ability to lead.

10. Though Michels confines his particular analysis to political parties the law of oligarchy is intended to have general application to all organization including the organization of the state as such. The majority will never rule despite the formal apparatus of universal suffrage and the myths of majority will. Democracy in the sense of the rule of the whole people or of the majority is impossible. In any democracy the major decisions will be taken by a powerful oligarchy. But Michels comes round to a limited defence of democracy. It allows the emergence of a number of rival parties—each led by an oligarchy—whose competition ensures a certain amount of indirect influence to the people whose support they must cultivate. The democratic tendency restrains but cannot prevent the oligarchical. As with Mosca elitism makes a compromise with pluralism when democracy is defined in terms of the competition between oligarchies.

Exercise 24. Does Democracy Require Affluence?

Modern social scientists commonly operate on the assumption that political forms, such as democracy and despotism, are by-products of underlying social forms. In other words they are alternative "superstructures" arising from alternative social "structures." A common subsidiary assumption is that the presence, the durability, the extent, and/or the stability of political democracy depends heavily on the scale of economic development, or general material prosperity, in host societies. A specific proposition related to these assumptions is that the life-chances of the democracy vary proportionally and positively with the level of economic development. The following selection is an adaptation of a celebrated attempt to test the latter proposition systematically.

Your assignment is to comment critically, concisely, and constructively on the functional relations between "economic development" and democracy, according to Lipset's study. You will find a great many points that warrant discussion. You should concentrate on the central points—the correlations that are shown and the causal inferences that might be derived therefrom. You may wish to begin with a brief, accurate sketch of what Lipset undertakes to show and what he claims to have shown. Certainly you need to identify and appraise the evidence presented and the use made of it. Pay particular attention to the propriety of what is said in paragraph II.3 in light of the data given and the methods used in Table 2.

Seymour Martin Lipset

Economic Development and Democracy*

I. Introduction

I. 1. Democracy in a complex society may be defined as a political system which supplies regular constitutional opportunities for changing the governing officials, and a social mechanism which permits the largest possible part of the population to influence major decisions by choosing among contenders for political office.

I. 2. This definition . . . implies a number of specific conditions: (1) a "political formula" or body of beliefs specifying which institutions—political parties, a free press, and so forth—are legitimate (accepted as proper by all); (2) one set of political leaders in office; and (3) one or more sets of recognized leaders attempting to gain office.

I. 3. The need for these conditions is clear. *First,* if a political system is not characterized by a value system allowing the peaceful "play" of power, democracy becomes chaotic. This has been the problem faced by many Latin-American states. *Second,* if the outcome of the political game is not the periodic awarding of effective authority to one group, unstable and irresponsible government rather than democracy will result. This state of affairs existed in pre-Fascist Italy, and through much, though not all, of the history of the Third and Fourth French Republics, which were characterized by weak coalition governments, often formed among parties having major interest and value conflicts with each other. *Third,* if the conditions for perpetuating an effective opposition do not exist, the authority of the officials in power will steadily increase, and popular influence on policy

*Abridged by permission from "Some Social Requisites of Democracy: Economic Development and Political Legitimacy," *The American Political Science Review,* vol. 53, no. 1, 1959, pp. 69–105. Most of the footnotes have been deleted. The roman numerals have been added.

will be at a minimum. This is the situation in all one-party states, and by general agreement, at least in the West, these are dictatorships.

I. 4. This . . . chapter will consider [a societal characteristic which bears] heavily on the problem of stable democracy: economic development. . . . Since most countries which lack an enduring tradition of political democracy lie in the underdeveloped sections of the world [Max] Weber may have been right when he suggested that modern democracy in its clearest form can occur only under capitalist industrialization. However, an extremely high correlation between such things as income, education, and religion, on the one hand, and democracy, on the other, in any given society should not be anticipated even on theoretical grounds because, to the extent that the political subsystem of the society operates autonomously, a political form may persist under conditions normally adverse to the *emergence* of that form. Or a political form may develop because of a syndrome of unique historical factors even though the society's major characteristics favor another form. Germany is an example of a nation where growing industrialization, urbanization, wealth, and education favored the establishment of a democratic system, but in which a series of adverse historical events prevented democracy from securing legitimacy and thus weakened its ability to withstand crisis.

I. 5. Key historical events may account for *either* the persistence *or* the failure of democracy in any particular society by starting a process which increases (or decreases) the likelihood that at the next critical point in the country's history democracy will win out again. Once established, a democratic political system "gathers momentum" and creates social supports (institutions) to ensure its continued existence. Thus a "premature" democracy which survives will do so by (among other things) facilitating the growth of other conditions conducive to democracy, such as universal literacy, or autonomous private organizations. In this chapter I am primarily concerned with the social conditions like education which serve to *support* democratic political systems, and I will not deal in detail with the internal mechanisms like the specific rules of the political game which serve to *maintain* them.

I. 6. A comparative study of complex social systems must necessarily deal rather summarily with the particular historical features of any one society. However, the deviation of a given nation from a particular aspect of democracy is not too important, as long as the definitions used cover the great majority of nations which are considered democratic or undemocratic. The precise dividing line between "more democratic" and "less democratic" is also not basic, since presumably democracy is not a unitary quality of a social system, but a complex of characteristics which may be ranked in many different ways. For this reason I have divided the countries under consideration into general categories, rather than attempting to rank them from highest to lowest, although even here such countries as Mexico pose problems.

I. 7. Efforts to classify all countries raised a number of problems. To reduce some of the complications introduced by the sharp variations in political practices in different parts of the earth I have concentrated on differences among countries

Political Forms: Democracy   49

within the same political culture areas. The two best areas for such internal comparison are Latin America, and Europe and the English-speaking countries. More limited comparisons can also be made among the Asian states and among the Arab countries.

I. 8. The main criteria used to define European democracies are the uninterrupted continuation of political democracy since World War I *and* the absence over the past twenty-five years of a major political movement opposed to the democratic "rules of the game."[1] The somewhat less stringent criterion for Latin America is whether a given country has had a history of more or less free elections for most of the post–World War I period.[2] Where in Europe we look for stable democracies, in South America we look for countries which have not had fairly constant dictatorial rule (see Table 1).

Table 1. Classification of European, English-speaking, and Latin-American Nations by Degree of Stable Democracy

European and English-speaking nations		Latin-American nations	
Stable democracies	Unstable democracies and dictatorships	Democracies and unstable dictatorships	Stable dictatorships
Australia	Albania	Argentina	Bolivia
Belgium	Austria	Brazil	Cuba
Canada	Bulgaria	Chile	Dominican Republic
Denmark	Czechoslovakia	Columbia	Ecuador
Ireland	Finland	Costa Rica	El Salvador
Luxembourg	France	Mexico	Guatemala
Netherlands	Germany	Uruguay	Haiti
New Zealand	Greece		Honduras
Norway	Hungary		Nicaragua
Sweden	Iceland		Panama
Switzerland	Italy		Paraguay
United Kingdom	Poland		Peru
United States	Portugal		Venezuela
	Rumania		
	Spain		
	U.S.S.R.		
	Yugoslavia		

[1] The latter requirement means that no totalitarian movement, either fascist or communist, received 20 percent of the vote during this time. Acutally all the European nations falling on the democratic side of the continuum had totalitarian movements which secured less than 7 percent of the vote.

[2] The historian Arthur P. Whitaker has summarized the judgments of experts on Latin America to be that "the countries which have approximated most closely to the democratic ideal have been . . . Argentina, Brazil, Chile, Columbia, Costa Rica, and Uruguay." See "The Pathology of Democracy in Latin America: A Historian's Point of View," *American Political Science Review*, 44 (1950), pp. 101–118. To this group I have added Mexico. Mexico has allowed freedom of the press, of assembly, and of organization to opposition parties, although there is good evidence that it does not allow them the opportunity to win elections since ballots are counted by the incumbents. The existence of opposition groups, contested elections, and adjustments among the various factions of the governing *Partido Revolucionario Institucional* does introduce a considerable element of popular influence in the system.

II. Economic Development in Europe and the Americas

II. 1. Perhaps the most common generalization linking political systems to other aspects of society has been that democracy is related to the state of economic development. The more well-to-do a nation, the greater the chances that it will sustain democracy. From Aristotle down to the present, men have argued that only in a wealthy society in which relatively few citizens lived at the level of real poverty could there be a situation in which the mass of the population intelligently participate in politics and develop the self-restraint necessary to avoid succumbing to the appeals of irresponsible demagogues. A society divided between a large impoverished mass and a small favored elite results either in oligarchy (dictatorial rule of the small upper stratum) or in tyranny (popular-based dictatorship). To give these two political forms modern labels, tyranny's face today is communism or Peronism; while oligarchy appears in the traditionalist dictatorships found in parts of Latin America, Thailand, Spain, or Portugal.

II. 2. To test this hypothesis concretely, I have used various indices of economic development—wealth, industrialization, urbanization, and education—and computed averages (means) for the countries which have been classified as more or less democratic in the Anglo-Saxon world and Europe, and in Latin America.

II. 3. In each case, the average wealth, degree of industrialization and urbanization, and level of education is much higher for the more democratic countries, as the data in Table 2 indicate. If I had combined Latin America and Europe in one table, the differences would have been even greater.

II. 4. The main indices of *wealth* used are per capita income, number of persons per motor vehicle and thousands of persons per physician, and the number of radios, telephones, and newspapers per thousand persons. The differences are

Table 2. A Comparison of European, English-speaking, and Latin-American Countries, Divided into Two Groups, "More Democratic" and "Less Democratic," by Indices of Wealth, Industrialization, Education, and Urbanization

A. Indices of Wealth

Means	Per capita income	Thousands of persons per doctor	Persons per motor vehicle
European and English-speaking Stable Democracies	U.S.$ 695	.86	17
European and English-speaking Unstable Democracies and Dictatorships	308	1.4	143
Latin-American Democracies and Unstable Dictatorships	171	2.1	99
Latin-American Stable Dictatorships	119	4.4	274

Political Forms: Democracy

Ranges	Per capita income	Thousands of persons per doctor	Persons per motor vehicle
European Stable Democracies	420–1,453	.7–1.2	3–62
European Dictatorships	128–482	.6–4	10–538
Latin-American Democracies	112–346	.8–3.3	31–174
Latin-American Stable Dictatorships	40–331	1.0–10.8	38–428

Means	Telephones per 1,000 persons	Radios per 1,000 persons	Newspaper copies per 1,000 persons
European and English-speaking Stable Democracies	205	350	341
European and English-speaking Unstable Democracies and Dictatorships	58	160	167
Latin-American Democracies and Unstable Dictatorships	25	85	102
Latin-American Stable Dictatorships	10	43	43

Ranges			
European Stable Democracies	43–400	160–995	242–570
European Dictatorships	7–196	42–307	46–390
Latin-American Democracies	12–58	38–148	51–233
Latin-American Stable Dictatorships	1–24	4–154	4–111

B. Indices of Industrialization

Means	Percentage of males in agriculture	Per capita energy consumed
European Stable Democracies	21	3.6
European Dictatorships	41	1.4
Latin-American Democracies	52	.6
Latin-American Stable Dictatorships	67	.25

Ranges		
European Stable Democracies	6–46	1.4–7.8
European Dictatorships	16–60	.27–3.2
Latin-American Democracies	30–63	.30–0.9
Latin-American Stable Dictatorships	46–87	.02–1.27

Table 2 — Continued

C. Indices of Education

Means	Percentage literate	Primary education enrollment per 1,000 persons	Post-primary enrollment per 1,000 persons	Higher education enrollment per 1,000 persons
European Stable Democracies	96	134	44	4.2
European Dictatorships	85	121	22	3.5
Latin-American Democracies	74	101	13	2.0
Latin-American Dictatorships	46	72	8	1.3
Ranges				
European Stable Democracies	95–100	96–179	19–83	1.7–17.83
European Dictatorships	55–98	61–165	8–37	1.6–6.1
Latin-American Democracies	48–87	75–137	7–27	.7–4.6
Latin-American Dictatorships	11–76	11–149	3–24	.2–3.1

D. Indices of Urbanization

Means	Percent in cities over 20,000	Percent in cities over 100,000	Percent in metropolitan areas
European Stable Democracies	43	28	38
European Dictatorships	24	16	23
Latin-American Democracies	28	22	26
Latin-American Stable Dictatorships	17	12	15
Ranges			
European Stable Democracies	28–54	17–51	22–56
European Dictatorships	12–44	6–33	7–49
Latin-American Democracies	11–48	13–37	17–44
Latin-American Stable Dictatorships	5–36	4–22	7–26

[Sources: Lipset derives these figures from various United Nations reports published during 1949–56. He explains "energy consumed" in the text of the chapter. He also stipulates that "not all the countries in each category were used for each calculation, as uniform data were not available for them all. For instance, the data available on Albania and East Germany are very sparse. The U.S.S.R. was left out because a large part of it is in Asia." *Eds.*]

striking on every score (see Table 2). In the more democratic European countries, there are 17 persons per motor vehicle compared to 143 for the less democratic. In the less dictatorial Latin-American countries there are 99 persons per motor vehicle versus 274 for the more dictatorial.[3] Income differences for the groups are also sharp, dropping from an average per capita income of $695 for the more democratic countries of Europe to $308 for the less democratic; the corresponding difference for Latin America is from $171 to $119. The ranges are equally consistent, with the lowest per capita income in each group falling in the "less democratic" category, and the highest in the "more democratic."

II. 5.   *Industrialization,* to which indices of wealth are of course clearly related, is measured by the percentage of employed males in agriculture and the per capita commercially produced "energy" being used in the country (measured in terms of tons of coal per person per year). Both of these show equally consistent results. The average percentage of employed males working in agriculture and related occupations was 21 in the "more democratic" European countries and 41 in the "less democratic"; 52 in the "less dictatorial" Latin-American countries and 67 in the "more dictatorial." The differences in per capita energy employed are equally large.

II. 6.   The degree of *urbanization* is also related to the existence of democracy. Three different indices of urbanization are available from data compiled by International Urban Research (Berkeley, California): the percentage of the population in communities of 20,000 and over, the percentage in communities of 100,000 and over, and the percentage residing in standard metropolitan areas. On all three of these indices the more democratic countries score higher than the less democratic for both of the areas under investigation.

II. 7.   Many people have suggested that the higher the *education* level of a nation's population, the better the chances for democracy, and the comparative data available support this proposition. The "more democratic" countries of Europe are almost entirely literate: the lowest has a rate of 96 percent; while the "less democratic" nations have an average rate of 85 percent. In Latin America the difference is between an average rate of 74 percent for the "less dictatorial" countries and 46 percent for the "more dictatorial."[4] The educational enrollment per thousand total population at three different levels—primary, postprimary, and higher educational—is equally consistently related to the degree of democracy. The tremendous disparity is shown by the extreme cases of Haiti and the United States. Haiti has fewer children (11 per thousand) attending school in

---

[3] It must be remembered that these figures are means, compiled from census figures for the various countries. The data vary widely in accuracy, and there is no way of measuring the validity of compound calculated figures such as those presented here. The consistent direction of all these differences, and their large magnitude, is the main indication of validity.

[4] The pattern indicated by a comparison of the averages for each group of countries is sustained by the ranges (the high and low extremes) for each index. Most of the ranges overlap; that is, some countries which are in the "less democratic" category are higher on any given index than some which are "more democratic." It is noteworthy that in both Europe and Latin America, the nations which are lowest on any of the indices presented in the table are also in the "less democratic" category. Conversely, almost all countries which rank at the top of any of the indices are in the "more democratic" class.

the primary grades than the United States has attending colleges (almost 18 per thousand).

II. 8. The relationship between education and democracy is worth more extensive treatment since an entire philosophy of government has seen increased education as the basic requirement of democracy. As James Bryce wrote, with special reference to South America, "education, if it does not make men good citizens, makes it at least easier for them to become so." Education presumably broadens man's outlook, enables him to understand the need for norms of tolerance, restrains him from adhering to extremist doctrines, and increases his capacity to make rational electoral choices.

II. 9. The evidence on the contribution of education to democracy is even more direct and strong on the level of individual behavior *within* countries than it is in cross-national correlations. Data gathered by public opinion research agencies which have questioned people in different countries about their beliefs on tolerance for the opposition, their attitudes toward ethnic or racial minorities, and their feelings for multi-party as against one-party systems have showed that the most important single factor differentiating those giving democratic responses from the others has been education. The higher one's education, the more likely one is to believe in democratic values and support democratic practices. All the relevant studies indicate that education is more significant than either income or occupation.

II. 10. These findings should lead us to anticipate a far higher correlation between national levels of education and political practice than we in fact find. Germany and France have been among the best educated nations of Europe, but this by itself did not stabilize their democracies. It may be, however, that their educational level has served to inhibit other antidemocratic forces.

II. 11. If we cannot say that a "high" level of education is a *sufficient* condition for democracy, the available evidence suggests that it comes close to being a *necessary* one. In Latin America, where widespread illiteracy still exists, only one of all the nations in which more than half the population is illiterate—Brazil—can be included in the "more democratic" group.

II. 12. Lebanon, the one member of the Arab League which has maintained democratic institutions since World War II, is also by far the best educated (over 80 percent literacy). East of the Arab world, only two states, the Philippines and Japan, have since 1945 maintained democratic regimes without the presence of large antidemocratic parties. And these two countries, although lower than most European states in per capita income, are among the world's leaders in educational attainment. The Philippines actually rank second to the United States in the proportion of people attending high schools and universities, and Japan has a higher educational level than any European nation.

II. 13. Although the evidence has been presented separately, all the various aspects of economic development—industrialization, urbanization, wealth, and education—are so closely interrelated as to form one major factor which has the

Dependent variable	Multiple correlation coefficient
Urbanization	.61
Literacy	.91
Media Participation	.84
Political Participation	.82

II. 14. In the Middle East, Turkey and Lebanon score higher on most of these indices than do the other four countries analyzed, and Daniel Lerner, in reporting on the study, points out [in *The Passing of Traditional Society,* 1958] that the "great post-war events in Egypt, Syria, Jordan and Iran have been the violent struggles for the control of power—struggles notably absent in Turkey and Lebanon [until very recently] where the control of power has been decided by elections."

II. 15. Lerner further points out the effect of disproportionate development, in one area or another, for over-all stability, and the need for co-ordinated changes in all of these variables. Comparing urbanization and literacy in Egypt and Turkey, he concludes that although Egypt is far more urbanized than Turkey, it is not really "modernized," and does not even have an adequate base for modernization, because literacy has not kept pace. In Turkey, all of the several indices of modernization have kept pace with each other, with rising voting participation (36 percent in 1950), balanced by rising literacy, urbanization, etc. In Egypt, the cities are full of "homeless illiterates," who provide a ready audience for political mobilization in support of extremist ideologies. On Lerner's scale, Egypt should be twice as literate as Turkey, since it is twice as urbanized. The fact that it is only half as literate explains, for Lerner, the "imbalances" which "tend to become circular and to accelerate social disorganization," political as well as economic.

II. 16. Lerner introduces one important theoretical addition—the suggestion

---

[5] This statement is a "statistical" statement, which necessarily means that there will be many exceptions to the correlation. Thus we know that poorer people are more likely to vote for the Democratic or Labor parties in the U.S. and England. The fact that a large minority of the lower strata vote for the more conservative party in these countries does not challenge the proposition that stratification position is a main determinant of party choice.

that these key variables in the modernization process may be viewed as historical phases, with democracy part of later developments, the "crowning institution of the participant society" (one of his terms for a modern industrial society). His view on the relations between these variables, seen as stages, is worth quoting at some length:

> The secular evolution of a participant society appears to involve a regular sequence of three phrases. Urbanization comes first, for cities alone have developed the complex of skills and resources which characterize the modern industrial economy. Within this urban matrix develop both of the attributes which distinguish the next two phases—literacy and media growth. There is a close reciprocal relationship between these, for the literate develop the media which in turn spread literacy. But, literacy performs the key function in the second phase. The capacity to read, at first acquired by relatively few people, equips them to perform the varied tasks required in the modernizing society. Not until the third phase, when the elaborate technology of industrial development is fairly well advanced, does a society begin to produce newspapers, radio networks, and motion pictures on a massive scale. This, in turn, accelerates the spread of literacy. Out of this interaction develop those institutions of participation (e.g., voting) which we find in all advanced modern societies.

II. 17. Lerner's thesis, that these elements of modernization are functionally interdependent, is by no means established by his data. But the material presented in this chapter offers an opportunity for research along these lines. Deviant cases, such as Egypt, where "lagging" literacy is associated with serious strains and potential upheaval, may also be found in Europe and Latin America, and their analysis—a task not attempted here—will further clarify the basic dynamics of modernization and the problem of social stability in the midst of institutional change.

III. Economic Development and the Class Struggle

III. 1. Economic development, producing increased income, greater economic security, and widespread higher education, largely determines the form of the "class struggle," by permitting those in the lower strata to develop longer time perspectives and more complex and gradualist views of politics. A belief in secular reformist gradualism can be the ideology of only a relatively well-to-do lower class. Striking evidence for this thesis may be found in the relationship between the patterns of working-class political action in different countries and the national income, a correlation that is almost startling in view of the many other cultural, historical, and juridical factors which affect the political life of nations.

III. 2. In the two wealthiest countries, the United States and Canada, not only are communist parties almost nonexistent but socialist parties have never been able to establish themselves as major forces. Among the eight next wealthiest countries — New Zealand, Switzerland, Sweden, United Kingdom, Denmark, Australia, Norway, Belgium, Luxembourg and Netherlands — all of whom had a per capita income of over $500 a year in 1949 (the last year for which standardized United Nations statistics exist), moderate socialism predominates as the form of leftist politics. In none of these countries did the Communists secure more than 7 percent of the vote, and the actual Communist party average among them has been about 4 percent. In the eight European countries which were below the $500 per capita income mark in 1949 — France, Iceland, Czechoslovakia, Finland, West Germany, Hungary, Italy, and Austria — and which have had at least one postwar democratic election in which both communist and noncommunist parties could compete, the Communist party has had more than 16 percent of the vote in six, and an over-all average of more than 20 percent in the eight countries as a group. The two low-income countries in which the Communists are weak — Germany and Austria — have both had direct experience with Soviet occupation.[6]

III. 3. Leftist extremism has also dominated working-class politics in two other European nations which belong to the under $500 per capital income group — Spain and Greece. In Spain before Franco, anarchism and left socialism were much stronger than moderate socialism; while in Greece, whose per capita income in 1949 was only $128, the Communists have always been much stronger than the socialists, and fellow-traveling parties have secured a large vote in recent years.

III. 4. The inverse relationship between national economic development as reflected by per capita income and the strength of Communists and other extremist groups among Western nations is seemingly stronger than the correlations between other national variables like ethnic or religious factors.[7] Two of the poorer nations with large Communist movements — Iceland and Finland — are Scandinavian and Lutheran. Among the Catholic nations of Europe, all the poor ones except Austria have large Communist or anarchist movements. The two wealthiest Catholic democracies — Belgium and Luxembourg — have few Communists. Though the French and Italian cantons of Switzerland are strongly affected by the cultural life of France and Italy, there are almost no Communists among the workers in these cantons, living in the wealthiest country in Europe.

III. 5. The relation between low per capita wealth and the precipitation of sufficient discontent to provide the social basis for political extremism is supported by a recent comparative polling survey of the attitudes of citizens of nine countries. Among these countries, feelings of personal security correlated with per capita income (.45) and with per capita food supply (.55). If satisfaction with one's country, as measured by responses to the question, "Which country in the

---

[6] It should be noted that before 1933–34, Germany had one of the largest Communist parties in Europe; while the Socialist party of Austria was the most left-wing and Marxist European party in the Socialist International.

[7] The relationship expressed above can be presented in another way. The seven European countries in which Communist or fellow-traveling parties have secured large votes in free elections had an average per capita income in 1949 of $330. The ten European countries in which the Communists have been a failure electorally had an average per capita income of $585.

world gives you the best chance of living the kind of life you would like to live?" is used as an index of the amount of discontent in a nation, then the relationship with economic wealth is even higher. The study reports a rank order correlation of .74 between per capita income and the degree of satisfaction with one's own country.[8]

III. 6. This does not mean that economic hardship or poverty *per se* is the main cause of radicalism. There is much evidence to sustain the argument that stable poverty in a situation in which individuals are not exposed to the possibilities of change breeds, if anything, conservatism.[9] Individuals whose experience limits their significant communications and interaction to others on the same level as themselves will, other conditions being equal, be more conservative than people who may be better off but who have been exposed to the possibilities of securing a better way of life. The dynamic in the situation would seem to be exposure to the possibility of a better way of life rather than poverty as such. As Karl Marx put it in a perceptive passage [in "Wage-Labor and Capital"]: "A house may be large or small; as long as the surrounding houses are equally small it satisfies all social demands for a dwelling. But if a palace arises beside the little house, the little house shrinks into a hut."

III. 7. With the growth of modern means of communication and transportation both within and among countries, it seems increasingly likely that the groups in the population that are poverty-stricken but are isolated from knowledge of better ways of life or unaware of the possibilities for improvement in their condition are becoming rarer and rarer, particularly in the urban areas of the Western world. One may expect to find such stable poverty only in tradition-dominated societies.

III. 8. Since position in a stratification system is always relative and gratification or deprivation is experienced in terms of being better or worse off than other people, it is not surprising that the lower classes in all countries, regardless of the wealth of the country, show various signs of resentment against the existing distribution of rewards by supporting political parties and other organizations which advocate some form of redistribution. The fact that the form which these political parties take in poorer countries is more extremist and radical than it is in wealthier ones is probably more related to the greater degree of inequality in such countries than to the fact that their poor are actually poorer in absolute terms. A comparative study of wealth distribution by the United Nations "suggest[s] that the richest fraction of the population (the richest 10th, 5th, etc.) generally receive[s] a greater proportion of the total income in the less developed than in the more developed countries. The gap between the income of professional and semiprofessional personnel on the one hand and ordinary workers on the other is much wider in the poorer than in the wealthier countries. Among manual workers, "there seems to be a greater wage discrepancy between skilled and unskilled

---

[8] William Buchanan and Hadley Cantril, *How Nations See Each Other* (Urbana: University of Illinois Press, 1953), p. 35.

[9] See Emile Durkheim, *Suicide: A Study in Sociology* (Glencoe: The Free Press, 1951), pp. 253–54; see also Daniel Bell, "The Theory of Mass Society," *Commentary*, 22 (1956), p. 80.

workers in the less developed countries. In contrast the leveling process, in several of the developed countries at least, has been facilitated by the over-all increase of national income . . . not so much by reduction of the income of the relatively rich as by the faster growth of the income of the relatively poor."

III. 9. The distribution of consumption goods also tends to become more equitable as the size of national income increases. The wealthier a country, the larger the proportion of its population which owns automobiles, telephones, bathtubs, refrigerating equipment, and so forth. Where there is a dearth of goods, the sharing of such goods must inevitably be less equitable than in a country in which there is relative abundance. For example, the number of people who can afford automobiles, washing machines, decent housing, telephones, good clothes, or have their children complete high school or go to college still represents only a small minority of the population in many European countries. The great national wealth of the United States or Canada, or even to a lesser extent the Australasian Dominions or Sweden, means that there is relatively little difference between the standards of living of adjacent social classes, and that even classes which are far apart in the social structure will enjoy more nearly similar consumption patterns than will comparable classes in Southern Europe. To a Southern European, and to an even greater extent to the inhabitant of one of the "underdeveloped" countries, social stratification is characterized by a much greater distinction in ways of life, with little overlap in the goods the various strata own or can afford to purchase. It may be suggested, therefore, that the wealthier a country, the less is status inferiority experienced as a major source of deprivation.

III. 10. Increased wealth and education also serve democracy by increasing the lower classes' exposure to cross-pressures which reduce their commitment to given ideologies and make them less receptive to extremist ones. The operation of this process will be discussed in more detail in the next chapter, but it means involving those strata in an integrated national culture as distinct from an isolated lower-class one.

III. 11. Marx believed that the proletariat was a revolutionary force because it had nothing to lose but its chains and could win the whole world. But [Alexis de] Tocqueville, analyzing the reasons why the lower strata in America supported the system, paraphrased and transposed Marx before Marx ever made his analysis by pointing out [in *Democracy in America*] that "only those who have nothing to lose ever revolt."

III. 12. Increased wealth also affects the political role of the middle class by changing the shape of the stratification structure from an elongated pyramid, with a large lower-class base, to a diamond with a growing middle class. A large middle class tempers conflict by rewarding moderate and democratic parties and penalizing extremist groups.

III. 13. The political values and style of the upper class, too, are related to national income. The poorer a country and the lower the absolute standard of living of the lower classes, the greater the pressure on the upper strata to treat the lower as vulgar, innately inferior, a lower caste beyond the pale of human society.

The sharp difference in the style of living between those at the top and those at the bottom makes this psychologically necessary. Consequently, the upper strata in such a situation tend to regard political rights for the lower strata, particularly the right to share power, as essentially absurd and immoral. The upper strata not only resist democracy themselves; their often arrogant political behavior serves to intensify extremist reactions on the part of the lower classes.

III. 14. The general income level of a nation also affects its receptivity to democratic norms. If there is enough wealth in the country so that it does not make too much difference whether some redistribution takes place, it is easier to accept the idea that it does not matter greatly which side is in power. But if loss of office means serious losses for major power groups, they will seek to retain or secure office by any means available. A certain amount of national wealth is likewise necessary to ensure a competent civil service. The poorer the country, the greater the emphasis on nepotism—support of kin and friends. And this in turn reduces the opportunity to develop the efficient bureaucracy which a modern democratic state requires.

III. 15. Intermediary organizations which act as sources of countervailing power seem to be similarly associated with national wealth. Tocqueville and other exponents of what has come to be known as the theory of the "mass society" have argued that a country without a multitude of organizations relatively independent of the central state power has a high dictatorial as well as revolutionary potential. Such organizations serve a number of functions: they inhibit the state or any single source of private power from dominating all political resources; they are a source of new opinions; they can be the means of communicating ideas, particularly opposition ideas, to a large section of the citizenry; they train men in political skills and so help to increase the level of interest and participation in politics. Although there are no reliable data on the relationship between national patterns of voluntary organization and national political systems, evidence from studies of individual behavior demonstrates that, regardless of other factors, men who belong to associations are more likely than others to give the democratic answer to questions concerning tolerance and party systems, to vote, or to participate actively in politics. Since the more well-to-do and better educated a man is, the more likely he is to belong to voluntary organizations, the propensity to form such groups seems to be a function of level of income and opportunities for leisure within given nations.

IV. The Politics of Rapid Economic Development

IV. 1. The association between economic development and democracy has led many Western statesmen and political commentators to conclude that the basic political problem of our day is produced by the pressure for rapid industrialization. If only the underdeveloped nations can be successfully started on the road to high productivity, the assumption runs, we can defeat the major threat to newly established democracies, their domestic Communists. In a curious way, this view marks the victory of economic determinism or vulgar Marxism within democratic political thought. Unfortunately for this theory, political extremism based on the lower classes, communism in particular, is not to be found only in low-income countries but also in newly industrializing nations. This correlation is not, of course, a recent phenomenon. In 1884, Engels noted that explicitly socialist labor movements had developed in Europe during periods of rapid industrial growth, and that these movements declined sharply during later periods of slower change.

IV. 2. The pattern of leftist politics in northern Europe in the first half of the twentieth century in countries whose socialist and trade-union movements are now relatively moderate and conservative illustrates this point. Wherever industrialization occurred *rapidly,* introducing sharp *discontinuities* between the pre-industrial and industrial situation, more rather than less extremist working-class movements emerged. In Scandinavia, for example, the variations among the socialist movements of Denmark, Sweden, and Norway can be accounted for in a large measure by the different timing and pace of industrialization, as the economist Walter Galenson has pointed out. The Danish Social Democratic movement and trade-unions have always been in the reformist, moderate, and relatively non-Marxist wing of the international labor movement. In Denmark, industrialization developed as a slow and gradual process. The rate of urban growth was also moderate, which had a good effect on urban working-class housing conditions. The slow growth of industry meant that a large proportion of Danish workers all during the period of industrialization were men who had been employed in industry for a long time, and, consequently, newcomers who had been pulled up from rural areas and who might have supplied the basis for extremist factions were always in a minority. The left-wing groups which gained some support in Denmark were based on the rapidly expanding industries.

IV. 3. In Sweden, on the other hand, manufacturing industry grew very rapidly from 1900 to 1914. This caused a sudden growth in the number of unskilled workers, largely recruited from rural areas, and the expansion of industrial rather than craft unions. Paralleling these developments in industry, a left-wing movement arose within the trade-unions and the Social Democratic party which opposed the moderate policies that both had developed before the great industrial expansion. A strong anarcho-syndicalist movement also emerged in this period. Here again, these aggressive left-wing movements were based on the rapidly expanding industries.

IV. 4. Norway, the last of the three Scandinavian countries to industrialize, had an even more rapid rate of growth. As a result of the emergence of hydroelectric power, the growth of an electrochemical industry, and the need for continued construction, Norway's industrial workers doubled between 1905 and 1920. And as in Sweden, this increase in the labor force meant that the traditional moderate craft-union movement was swamped by unskilled and semiskilled workers, most of whom were young migrants from rural areas. A left wing emerged within the Federation of Labor and the Labor party, capturing control of both in the latter stages of World War I. It should be noted that Norway was the only Western European country which was still in its phase of rapid industrialization when the Comintern was founded, and its Labor party was the only one which went over almost intact to the Communists.

IV. 5. In Germany before World War I, a revolutionary Marxist left wing, in large measure derived from workers in the rapidly growing industries, retained considerable support within the Social Democratic party, while the more moderate sections of the party were based on the more stable established industries.

IV. 6. The most significant illustration of the relationship between rapid industrialization and working-class extremism is the Russian Revolution. In Czarist Russia, the industrial population jumped from 16 million in 1897 to 26 million in 1913. Trotsky in his *History of the Russian Revolution* has shown how an increase in the strike rate and in union militancy paralleled the growth of industry. It is probably not coincidental that two nations in Europe in which the revolutionary left gained control of the dominant section of the labor movement before 1920—Russia and Norway—were also countries in which the processes of rapid capital accumulation and basic industrialization were still going on.

IV. 7. The revolutionary socialist movements which arise in response to strains created by rapid industrialization decline, as Engels put it [in a letter to Karl Kautsky in November 1884], wherever "the transition to large-scale industry is more or less completed . . . [and] the conditions in which the proletariat is placed become stable." Such countries are, of course, precisely the industrialized nations where Marxism and revolutionary socialism exist today only as sectarian dogmas. In those nations of Europe where industrialization never occurred, or where it failed to build an economy of efficient large-scale industry with a high level of productivity and a constant increase in mass-consumption patterns, the conditions for the creation or perpetuation of extremist labor politics also exist.

IV. 8. A different type of extremism, based on the small entrepreneurial classes (both urban and rural), has emerged in the less developed and often culturally backward sectors of more industrialized societies. The social base of classic fascism seems to arise from the ever present vulnerability of part of the middle class, particularly small businessmen and farm owners, to large-scale capitalism and a powerful labor movement. . . .

IV. 9. It is obvious that the conditions related to stable democracy discussed here are most readily found in the countries of northwest Europe and their English-speaking offspring in America and Australasia; and it has been suggested, by Weber among others, that a historically unique concatenation of elements produced both democracy and capitalism in this area. Capitalist economic development, the basic argument runs, had its greatest opportunity in a Protestant society and created the burgher class whose existence was both a catalyst and a necessary condition for democracy. Protestantism's emphasis on individual responsibility furthered the emergence of democratic values in these countries and resulted in an alignment between the burghers and the throne which preserved the monarchy and extended the acceptance of democracy among the conservative strata. Men may question whether any aspect of this interrelated cluster of economic development, Protestantism, monarchy, gradual political change, legitimacy, and democracy is primary, but the fact remains that the cluster does hang together.

V. Methodological Appendix

V. 1. The approach in this chapter is implicitly different from some other studies which have attempted to handle social phenomena on a total societal level, and it may be useful to make explicit some of the methodological postulates underlying this presentation.

V. 2. Complex characteristics of a social system, such as democracy, the degree of bureaucratization, the type of stratification system, have usually been handled by either a reductionist or an "ideal-type" approach. The former dismisses the possibility of considering these characteristics as system-attributes as such, and maintains that the qualities of individual actions are the sum and substance of sociological categories. For this school of thought, the extent of democratic attitudes, or of bureaucratic behavior, or the numbers and types of prestige or power rankings, constitute the essence of the meaning of the attributes of democracy, bureaucracy, or class.

V. 3. The "ideal-type" approach starts from a similar assumption, but reaches an opposite conclusion. The similar assumption is that societies are a complex order of phenomena, exhibiting such a degree of internal contradiction that generalizations about them as a whole must necessarily constitute a constructed representation of selected elements, stemming from the particular concerns and perspectives of the scientist. The opposite conclusion is that abstractions of the order of "democracy" or "bureaucracy" have no necessary connection with states or qualities of complex social systems which actually exist, but comprise collections of attributes which are logically interrelated but characteristic in their entirety of no existing society. An example is Weber's concept of "bureaucracy," comprising a set of offices which are not "owned" by the officeholder, continuously maintained files of records, functionally specified duties, etc.; so is the common definition of democracy in political science, which postulates individual political decisions based on rational knowledge of one's own ends and of the factual political situation.

V. 4. Criticism of such categories or ideal-types solely on the basis that they do not correspond to reality is irrelevant, because they are not intended to describe reality, but to provide a basis for comparing different aspects of reality with the consistently logical case. Often this approach is quite fruitful, and there is no intention here of substituting another in its place, but merely of presenting another possible way of conceptualizing complex characteristics of social systems, stemming from the multi-variate analysis pioneered by Paul Lazarsfeld and his colleagues on a quite different level of analysis.

V. 5. The point at which this approach differs is on the issue of whether generalized theoretical categories can be considered to have a valid relationship to characteristics of total social systems. The implication of the statistical data presented in this chapter on democracy, and the relations between democracy, economic development, and political legitimacy, is that there are aspects of total social systems which exist, can be stated in theoretical terms, can be compared with similar aspects of other systems, and, at the same time, are derivable from empirical data which can be checked (or questioned) by other researchers. This does not mean that situations contradicting the general relationship may not exist, or that at lower levels of social organization quite different characteristics may not be evident. For example, a country like the United States may be characterized as "democratic" on the national level, even though most secondary organizations within the country may not be democratic. On another level, a church may be characterized as an "unbureaucratic" organization compared to a corporation, even though important segments of the church organization may be as bureaucratized as the most bureaucratic parts of the corporation. On yet another level, it may be quite legitimate, for purposes of psychological evaluation of the total personality, to consider a certain individual "schizophrenic," even though under certain conditions he may not act schizophrenically. The point is that when comparisons are being made on a certain level of generalization, referring to the functioning of a total system (whether on a personality, group, organization, or society level), generalizations applicable to a total society have the same kind and degree of validity that those applicable to other systems have, and are subject to the same empirical tests. The lack of systematic and comparative study of several societies has obscured this point.

V. 6. This approach also stresses the view that complex characteristics of a total system have multi-variate causation and consequences, in so far as the characteristic has some degree of autonomy within the system. Bureaucracy and urbanization, as well as democracy, have many causes and consequences, in this sense.

V. 7. From this point of view, it would be difficult to identify any *one* factor crucially associated with, or "causing," any complex social characteristic. Rather, all such characteristics (and this is a methodological assumption to guide research, and not a substantive point) are considered to have multi-variate causation, and consequences. The point may be clarified by a diagram of some of the

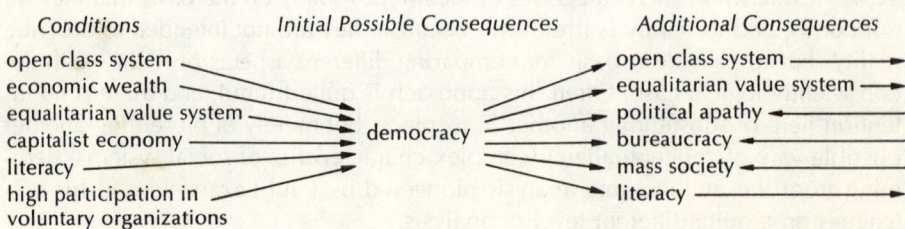

possible connections between democracy, the initial conditions associated with its emergence, and the consequences of an existent democratic system.

V. 8. The appearance of a factor on both sides of "democracy" implies that it is both an initial condition of democracy, and that democracy, once established, sustains that characteristic of the society—an open class system, for example. On the other hand, some of the initial consequences of democracy, such as bureaucracy, may have the effect of *undermining* democracy, as the reversing arrows indicate. Appearance of a factor to the right of democracy does not mean that democracy "causes" its appearance, but merely that democracy is an initial condition which favors its development. Similarly, the hypothesis that bureaucracy is one of the consequences of democracy does not imply that democracy is the sole cause, but rather that a democratic system has the effect of encouraging the development of a certain type of bureaucracy under other conditions which have to be stated if bureaucracy is the focus of the research problem. This diagram is not intended as a complete model of the general social conditions associated with the emergence of democracy, but as a way of clarifying the methodological point concerning the multi-variate character of relationships in a total social system.

V. 9. Thus, in a multi-variate system, the focus may be upon any element, and its conditions and consequences may be stated without the implication that we have arrived at a complete theory of the necessary and sufficient conditions of its emergence. This chapter does not attempt a *new* theory of democracy, but only the formalizing and empirical testing of certain sets of relationships implied by traditional theories of democracy.

Social Forms: Equality

Since the time of the French Revolution in 1789, if not before, "equality" has been a fighting word. Men have furiously debated the essence, the desirability, and the feasibility of equality in relations between human beings. Generally they have agreed that equality is and has been the exception rather than the norm in human relations. They have differed passionately about whether equality is *necessarily* an exceptional condition.

Exercise 25. Is Equality Attainable?

The following essay conveys how modern sociologists and anthropologists have pondered the meaning, the incidence, the consequences, and—most pointedly—the feasibility of equality. We can properly describe this essay as a minor classic in broad-gauged theorizing by modern social scientists. Although it appeared more than 25 years ago, the essay is still widely read and cited.

Your assignment is to examine this work critically, concisely, and constructively. In so doing you should adopt, to the best of your ability, the outlook of a champion of equality. Assume that your readers share your prejudice in favor of equality but also are reasonable people who have read this essay and have been discomfited by it. They need reassurance, if not direct rebuttal. Your critique should briefly but accurately sketch the main lines of argument unfolded in the essay and should formulate plausible lines of counterargument that are reassuring to exponents of equality.

Kingsley Davis and Wilbert E. Moore

*Some Principles of Stratification**

I. Introduction

I. 1. In a previous paper some concepts for handling the phenomena of social inequality were presented.[1] In the present paper a further step in stratification theory is undertaken—an attempt to show the relationship between stratification and the rest of social order.[2] Starting from the proposition that no society is "classless," or unstratified, an effort is made to explain, in functional terms, the universal necessity which calls forth stratification in any social system. Next, an attempt is made to explain the roughly uniform distribution of prestige as between the major types of positions in every society. Since, however, there occur between one society and another great differences in the degree and kind of stratification, some attention is also given to the varieties of social inequality and the variable factors that give rise to them.

I. 2. Clearly, the present task requires two different lines of analysis—one to understand the universal, the other to understand the variable features of stratification. Naturally each line of inquiry aids the other and is indispensable, and in the treatment that follows the two will be interwoven, although, because of space limitations, the emphasis will be on the universals.

I. 3. Throughout, it will be necessary to keep in mind one thing—namely, that the discussion relates to the system of positions, not to the individuals occupying those positions. It is one thing to ask why different positions carry different degrees of prestige, and quite another to ask how certain individuals get

---

*Reprinted by permission from *The American Sociological Review*, vol. 10, no. 2, 1945, pp. 242–49.

[1] Kingsley Davis, "A Conceptual Analysis of Stratification," *American Sociological Review*, 7:309–321, June, 1942.

[2] The writers regret (and beg indulgence) that the present essay, a condensation of a longer study, covers so much in such short space that adequate evidence and qualification cannot be given and that as a result what is actually very tentative is presented in an unfortunately dogmatic manner.

into those positions. Although, as the argument will try to show, both questions are related, it is essential to keep them separate in our thinking. Most of the literature on stratification has tried to answer the second question (particularly with regard to the ease or difficulty of mobility between strata) without tackling the first. The first question, however, is logically prior and, in the case of any particular individual or group, factually prior.

II. The Functional Necessity of Stratification

II. 1. Curiously, however, the main functional necessity explaining the universal presence of stratification is precisely the requirement faced by any society of placing and motivating individuals in the social structure. As a functioning mechanism a society must somehow distribute its members in social positions and induce them to perform the duties of these positions. It must thus concern itself with motivation at two different levels: to instill in the proper individuals the desire to fill certain positions, and, once in these positions, the desire to perform the duties attached to them. Even though the social order may be relatively static in form, there is a continuous process of metabolism as new individuals are born into it, shift with age, and die off. Their absorption into the positional system must somehow be arranged and motivated. This is true whether the system is competitive or non-competitive. A competitive system gives greater importance to the motivation to achieve positions, whereas a non-competitive system gives perhaps greater importance to the motivation to perform the duties of the positions; but in any system both types of motivation are required.

II. 2. If the duties associated with the various positions were all equally pleasant to the human organism, all equally important to societal survival, and all equally in need of the same ability or talent, it would make no difference who got into which positions, and the problem of social placement would be greatly reduced. But actually it does make a great deal of difference who gets into which positions, not only because some positions are inherently more agreeable than others, but also because some require special talents or training and some are functionally more important than others. Also, it is essential that the duties of the positions be performed with the diligence that their importance requires. Inevitably, then, a society must have, first, some kind of rewards that it can use as inducements, and, second, some way of distributing these rewards differentially according to positions. The rewards and their distribution become a part of the social order, and thus give rise to stratification.

II. 3. One may ask what kind of rewards a society has at its disposal in distributing its personnel and securing essential services. It has, first of all, the things that contribute to sustenance and comfort. It has, second, the things that contribute to humor and diversion. And it has, finally, the things that contribute to self respect and ego expansion. The last, because of the peculiarly social character of the self, is largely a function of the opinion of others, but it nonetheless ranks in importance with the first two. In any social system all three kinds of rewards must be dispensed differentially according to positions.

II. 4. In a sense the rewards are "built into" the position. They consist in the "rights" associated with the position, plus what may be called its accompaniments or perquisites. Often the rights, and sometimes the accompaniments, are functionally related to the duties of the position. (Rights as viewed by the incumbent are usually duties as viewed by other members of the community.) However, there may be a host of subsidiary rights and perquisites that are not essential to the function of the position and have only an indirect and symbolic connection with its duties, but which still may be of considerable importance in inducing people to seek the positions and fulfil the essential duties.

II. 5. If the rights and perquisites of different positions in a society must be unequal, then the society must be stratified, because that is precisely what stratification means. Social inequality is thus an unconsciously evolved device by which societies insure that the most important positions are conscientiously filled by the most qualified persons. Hence every society, no matter how simple or complex, must differentiate persons in terms of both prestige and esteem, and must therefore possess a certain amount of institutionalized inequality.

II. 6. It does not follow that the amount or type of inequality need be the same in all societies. This is largely a function of factors that will be discussed presently.

III. The Two Determinants of Positional Rank

III. 1. Granting the general function that inequality subserves, one can specify the two factors that determine the relative rank of different positions. In general those positions convey the best reward, and hence have the highest rank, which (a) have the greatest importance for the society and (b) require the greatest training or talent. The first factor concerns function and is a matter of relative significance; the second concerns means and is a matter of scarcity.

III. 2. *Differential Functional Importance*. Actually a society does not need to reward positions in proportion to their functional importance. It merely needs to give sufficient reward to them to insure that they will be filled competently. In other words, it must see that less essential positions do not compete successfully with more essential ones. If a position is easily filled, it need not be heavily rewarded, even though important. On the other hand, if it is important but hard to fill, the reward must be high enough to get it filled anyway. Functional importance is therefore a necessary but not a sufficient cause of high rank being assigned to a position.[3]

---

[3] Unfortunately, functional importance is difficult to establish. To use the position's prestige to establish it, as is often unconsciously done, constitutes circular reasoning from our point of view. There are, however, two independent clues: (a) the degree to which a position is functionally unique, there being no other positions that can perform the same function satisfactorily; (b) the degree to

III. 3. *Differential Scarcity of Personnel.* Practically all positions, no matter how acquired, require some form of skill or capacity for performance. This is implicit in the very notion of position, which implies that the incumbent must, by virtue of his incumbency, accomplish certain things.

III. 4. There are, ultimately, only two ways in which a person's qualifications come about: through inherent capacity or through training. Obviously, in concrete activities both are always necessary, but from a practical standpoint the scarcity may lie primarily in one or the other, as well as in both. Some positions require innate talents of such high degree that the persons who fill them are bound to be rare. In many cases, however, talent is fairly abundant in the population but the training process is so long, costly, and elaborate that relatively few can qualify. Modern medicine, for example, is within the mental capacity of most individuals, but a medical education is so burdersome and expensive that virtually none would undertake it if the position of the M.D. did not carry a reward commensurate with the sacrifice.

III. 5. If the talents required for a position are abundant and the training easy, the method of acquiring the position may have little to do with its duties. There may be, in fact, a virtually accidental relationship. But if the skills required are scarce by reason of the rarity of talent or the costliness of training the position, if functionally important, must have an attractive power that will draw the necessary skills in competition with other positions. This means, in effect, that the position must be high in the social scale—must command great prestige, high salary, ample leisure, and the like.

III. 6. *How Variations Are to Be Understood.* In so far as there is a difference between one system of stratification and another, it is attributable to whatever factors affect the two determinants of differential reward—namely, functional importance and scarcity of personnel. Positions important in one society may not be important in another, because the conditions faced by the societies, or their degree of internal development, may be different. The same conditions, in turn, may affect the question of scarcity; for in some societies the stage of development, or the external situation, may wholly obviate the necessity of certain kinds of skill or talent. Any particular system of stratification, then, can be understood as a product of the special conditions affecting the two aforementioned grounds of differential reward.

---

which other positions are dependent on the one in question. Both clues are best exemplified in organized systems of positions built around one major function. Thus, in most complex societies the religious, political, economic, and educational functions are handled by distinct structures not easily interchangeable. In addition, each structure possesses many different positions, some clearly dependent on, if not subordinate to, others. In sum, when an institutional nucleus becomes differentiated around one main function, and at the same time organizes a large portion of the population into its relationships, the *key* positions in it are of the highest functional importance. The absence of such specialization does not prove functional unimportance, for the whole society may be relatively unspecialized; but it is safe to assume that the more important functions receive the first and clearest structural differentiation.

IV. Major Societal Functions and Stratification

IV. 1.   *Religion.* The reason why religion is necessary is apparently to be found in the fact that human society achieves its unity primarily through the possession by its members of certain ultimate values and ends in common. Although these values and ends are subjective, they influence behavior, and their integration enables the society to operate as a system. Derived neither from inherited nor from external nature, they have evolved as a part of culture by communication and moral pressure. They must, however, appear to the members of the society to have some reality, and it is the role of religious belief and ritual to supply and reinforce this appearance of reality. Through belief and ritual the common ends and values are connected with an imaginary world symbolized by concrete sacred objects, which world in turn is related in a meaningful way to the facts and trials of the individual's life. Through the worship of the sacred objects and the beings they symbolize, and the acceptance of supernatural prescriptions that are at the same time codes of behavior, a powerful control over human conduct is exercised, guiding it along lines sustaining the institutional structure and conforming to the ultimate ends and values.

IV. 2.   If this conception of the role of religion is true, one can understand why in every known society the religious activities tend to be under the charge of particular persons, who tend thereby to enjoy greater rewards than the ordinary societal member. Certain of the rewards and special privileges may attach to only the highest religious functionaries, but others usually apply, if such exists, to the entire sacerdotal class.

IV. 3.   Moreover, there is a peculiar relation between the duties of the religious official and the special privileges he enjoys. If the supernatural world governs the destinies of men more ultimately than does the real world, its earthly representative, the person through whom one may communicate with the supernatural, must be a powerful individual. He is a keeper of sacred tradition, a skilled performer of the ritual, and an interpreter of lore and myth. He is in such close contact with the gods that he is viewed as possessing some of their characteristics. He is, in short, a bit sacred, and hence free from some of the more vulgar necessities and controls.

IV. 4.   It is no accident, therefore, that religious functionaries have been associated with the very highest positions of power, as in theocratic regimes. Indeed, looking at it from this point of view, one may wonder why it is that they do not get *entire* control over their societies. The factors that prevent this are worthy of note.

IV. 5.   In the first place, the amount of technical competence necessary for the performance of religious duties is small. Scientific or artistic capacity is not required. Anyone can set himself up as enjoying an intimate relation with deities, and nobody can successfully dispute him. Therefore, the factor of scarcity of personnel does not operate in the technical sense.

IV. 6.   One may assert, on the other hand, that religious ritual is often elaborate and religious lore abstruse, and that priestly ministrations require tact, if not intelligence. This is true, but the technical requirements of the profession are for the most part adventitious, not related to the end in the same way that science is related to air travel. The priest can never be free from competition, since the criteria of whether or not one has genuine contact with the supernatural are never strictly clear. It is this competition that debases the priestly position below what might be expected at first glance. That is why priestly prestige is highest in those societies where membership in the profession is rigidly controlled by the priestly guild itself. That is why, in part at least, elaborate devices are utilized to stress the identification of the person with his office—spectacular costume, abnormal conduct, special diet, segregated residence, celibacy, conspicuous leisure, and the like. In fact, the priest is always in danger of becoming somewhat discredited—as happens in a secularized society—because in a world of stubborn fact, ritual and sacred knowledge alone will not grow crops or build houses. Furthermore, unless he is protected by a professional guild, the priest's identification with the supernatural tends to preclude his acquisition of abundant wordly goods.

IV. 7. As between one society and another it seems that the highest general position awarded the priest occurs in the medieval type of social order. Here there is enough economic production to afford a surplus, which can be used to support a numerous and highly organized priesthood; and yet the populace is unlettered and therefore credulous to a high degree. Perhaps the most extreme example is to be found in the Buddhism of Tibet, but others are encountered in the Catholicism of feudal Europe, the Inca regime of Peru, the Brahminism of India, and the Mayan priesthood of Yucatan. On the other hand, if the society is so crude as to have no surplus and little differentiation, so that every priest must be also a cultivator or hunter, the separation of the priestly status from the others has hardly gone far enough for priestly prestige to mean much. When the priest actually has high prestige under these circumstances, it is because he also performs other important functions (usually political and medical).

IV. 8. In an extremely advanced society built on scientific technology, the preisthood tends to lose status, because sacred tradition and supernaturalism drop into the background. The ultimate values and common ends of the society tend to be expressed in less anthropomorphic ways, by officials who occupy fundamentally political, economic, or educational rather than religious positions. Nevertheless, it is easily possible for intellectuals to exaggerate the degree to which the priesthood in a presumably secular milieu has lost prestige. When the matter is closely examined the urban proletariat, as well as the rural citizenry, proves to be surprisingly god-fearing and priest-ridden. No society has become so completely secularized as to liquidate entirely the belief in transcendental ends and supernatural entities. Even in a secularized society some system must exist for the integration of ultimate values, for their ritualistic expression, and for the emotional adjustments required by disappointment, death, and disaster.

IV. 9. *Government.* Like religion, government plays a unique and indispensable part in society. But in contrast to religion, which provides integration in terms of sentiments, beliefs, and rituals, it organizes the society in terms of law and authority. Furthermore, it orients the society to the actual rather than the unseen world.

IV. 10. The main functions of government are, internally, the ultimate enforcement of norms, the final arbitration of conflicting interests, and the overall planning and direction of society; and externally, the handling of war and diplomacy. To carry out these functions it acts as the agent of the entire people, enjoys a monopoly of force, and controls all individuals within its territory.

IV. 11. Political action, by definition, implies authority. An official can command because he has authority, and the citizen must obey because he is subject to that authority. For this reason stratification is inherent in the nature of political relationships.

IV. 12. So clear is the power embodied in political position that political inequality is sometimes thought to comprise all inequality. But it can be shown that there are other bases of stratification, that the following controls operate in practice to keep political power from becoming complete: (a) The fact that the actual holders of political office, and especially those determining top policy must necessarily be few in number compared to the total population. (b) The fact that the rulers represent the interest of the group rather than of themselves, and are therefore restricted in their behavior by rules and mores designed to enforce this limitation of interest. (c) The fact that the holder of political office has his authority by virtue of his office and nothing else, and therefore any special knowledge, talent, or capcity he may claim is purely incidental, so that he often has to depend upon others for technical assistance.

IV. 13. In view of these limiting factors, it is not strange that the rulers often have less power and prestige than a literal enumeration of their formal rights would lead one to expect.

IV. 14. *Wealth, Property, and Labor.* Every position that secures for its incumbent a livelihood is, by definition, economically rewarded. For this reason there is an economic aspect to those positions (e.g. political and religious) the main function of which is not economic. It therefore becomes convenient for the society to use unequal economic returns as a principal means of controlling the entrance of persons into positions and stimulating the performance of their duties. The amount of the economic return therefore becomes one of the main indices of social status.

IV. 15. It should be stressed, however, that a position does not bring power and prestige *because* it draws a high income. Rather, it draws a high income because it is functionally important and the available personnel is for one reason or another scarce. It is therefore superficial and erroneous to regard high income as the cause of a man's power and prestige, just as it is erroneous to think that a man's fever is the cause of his disease.[4]

---

[4] The symbolic rather than intrinsic role of income in social stratification has been succinctly summarized by Talcott Parsons, "An Analytical Approach to the Theory of Social Stratification," *American Journal of Sociology.* 45:841–862, May, 1940.

IV. 16. The economic source of power and prestige is not income primarily, but the ownership of capital goods (including patents, good will, and professional reputation). Such ownership should be distinguished from the possession of consumers' goods, which is an index rather than a cause of social standing. In other words, the ownership of producers' goods is properly speaking, a source of income like other positions, the income itself remaining an index. Even in situations where social values are widely commercialized and earnings are the readiest method of judging social position, income does not confer prestige on a position so much as it induces people to compete for the position. It is true that a man who has a high income as a result of one position may find this money helpful in climbing into another position as well, but this again reflects the effect of his initial, economically advantageous status, which exercises its influence through the medium of money.

IV. 17. In a system of private property in productive enterprise, an income above what an individual spends can give rise to possession of capital wealth. Presumably such possession is a reward for the proper management of one's finances originally and of the productive enterprise later. But as social differentiation becomes highly advanced and yet the institution of inheritance persists, the phenomenon of pure ownership, and reward for pure ownership, emerges. In such a case it is difficult to prove that the position is functionally important or that the scarcity involved is anything other than extrinsic and accidental. It is for this reason, doubtless, that the institution of private property in productive goods becomes more subject to criticism as social development proceeds toward industrialization. It is only this pure, that is, strictly legal and functionless ownership, however, that is open to attack; for some form of active ownership, whether private or public, is indispensable.

IV. 18. One kind of ownership of production goods consists in rights over the labor of others. The most extremely concentrated and exclusive of such rights are found in slavery, but the essential principle remains in serfdom, peonage, encomienda, and indenture. Naturally this kind of ownership has the greatest significance for stratification, because it necessarily entails an unequal relationship.

IV. 19. But property in capital goods inevitably introduces a compulsive element even into the nominally free contractual relationship. Indeed, in some respects the authority of the contractual employer is greater than that of the feudal landlord, inasmuch as the latter is more limited by traditional reciprocities. Even the classical economics recognized that competitors would fare unequally, but it did not pursue this fact to its necessary conclusion that, however it might be acquired, unequal control of goods and services must give unequal advantage to the parties to a contract.

IV. 20. *Technical Knowledge.* The function of finding means to single goals, without any concern with the choice between goals, is the exclusively technical sphere. The explanation of why positions requiring great technical skill receive fairly high rewards is easy to see, for it is the simplest case of the rewards being so distributed as to draw talent and motivate training. Why they seldom if ever receive the highest rewards is also clear: the importance of technical knowledge from a societal point of view is never so great as the integration of goals, which takes place on the religious, political, and economic levels. Since the technological level is concerned solely with means, a purely technical position must ultimately be subordinate to other positions that are religious, political, or economic in character.

IV. 21. Nevertheless, the distinction between expert and layman in any social order is fundamental, and cannot be entirely reduced to other terms. Methods of recruitment, as well as of reward, sometimes lead to the erroneous interpretation that technical positions are economically determined. Actually, however, the acquisition of knowledge and skill cannot be accomplished by purchase, although the opportunity to learn may be. The control of the avenues of training may inhere as a sort of property right in certain families or classes, giving them power and prestige in consequence. Such a situation adds an artificial scarcity to the natural scarcity of skills and talents. On the other hand, it is possible for an opposite situation to arise. The rewards of technical position may be so great that a condition of excess supply is created, leading to at least temporary devaluation of the rewards. Thus "unemployment in the learned professions" may result in a debasement of the prestige of those positions. Such adjustments and readjustments are constantly occurring in changing societies; and it is always well to bear in mind that the efficiency of a stratified structure may be affected by the modes of recruitment for positions. The social order itself, however, sets limits to the inflation or deflation of the prestige of experts: an over-supply tends to debase the rewards and discourage recruitment or produce revolution, whereas an under-supply tends to increase the rewards or weaken the society in competition with other societies.

IV. 22. Particular systems of stratification show a wide range with respect to the exact position of technically competent persons. This range is perhaps most evident in the degree of specialization. Extreme division of labor tends to create many specialists without high prestige since the training is short and the required native capacity relatively small. On the other hand it also tends to accentuate the high position of the true experts—scientists, engineers, and administrators—by increasing their authority relative to other functionally important positions. But the idea of a technocratic social order or a government or priesthood of engineers or social scientists neglects the limitations of knowledge and skills as a basic for performing social functions. To the extent that the social structure is truly specialized the prestige of the technical person must also be circumscribed.

V. Variation in Stratified Systems

V. 1. The generalized principles of stratification here suggested form a necessary preliminary to a consideration of types of stratified systems, because it is in terms of these principles that the types must be described. This can be seen by trying to delineate types according to certain modes of variation. For instance, some of the most important modes (together with the polar types in terms of them) seem to be as follows:

V. 2. (a) *The Degree of Specialization*. The degree of specialization affects the fineness and multiplicity of the gradations in power and prestige. It also influences the extent to which particular functions may be emphasized in the invidious system, since a given function cannot receive much emphasis in the hierarchy until it has achieved structural separation from the other functions. Finally, the amount of specialization influences the bases of selection. Polar types: *Specialized, Unspecialized*.

V. 3. (b) *The Nature of the Functional Emphasis*. In general when emphasis is put on sacred matters, a rigidity is introduced that tends to limit specialization and hence the development of technology. In addition, a brake is placed on social mobility, and on the development of bureaucracy. When the preoccupation with the sacred is withdrawn, leaving greater scope for purely secular preoccupations, a great development, and rise in status, of economic and technological positions seemingly takes place. Curiously, a concomitant rise in political position is not likely, because it has usually been allied with the religious and stands to gain little by the decline of the latter. It is also possible for a society to emphasize family functions—as in relatively undifferentiated societies where high mortality requires high fertility and kinship forms the main basis of social organization. Main types: *Familistic, Authoritarian* (*Theocratic* or sacred, and *Totalitarian* or secular), *Capitalistic*.

V. 4. (c) *The Magnitude of Invidious Differences*. What may be called the amount of social distance between positions, taking into account the entire scale, is something that should lend itself to quantitative measurement. Considerable differences apparently exist between different societies in this regard, and also between parts of the same society. Polar types: *Equalitarian, Inequalitarian*.

V. 5. (d) *The Degree of Opportunity*. The familiar question of the amount of mobility is different from the question of the comparative equality or inequality of rewards posed above, because the two criteria may vary independently up to a point. For instance, the tremendous divergences in monetary income in the United States are far greater than those found in primitive societies, yet the equality of opportunity to move from one rung to the other in the social scale may also be greater in the United States than in a hereditary tribal kingdom. Polar types: *Mobile* (open), *Immobile* (closed).

V. 6. (e) *The Degree of Stratum Solidarity*. Again, the degree of "class solidarity" (or the presence of specific organizations to promote class interests) may vary to some extent independently of the other criteria, and hence is an important principle in classifying systems of stratification. Polar types: *Class organized, Class unorganized*.

VI. External Conditions

VI. 1. What state any particular system of stratification is in with reference to each of these modes of variation depends on two things: (1) its state with reference to the other ranges of variation, and (2) the conditions outside the system of stratification which nevertheless influence that system. Among the latter are the following:

VI. 2. (a) *The Stage of Cultural Development.* As the cultural heritage grows, increased specialization becomes necessary, which in turn contributes to the enhancement of mobility, a decline of stratum solidarity, and a change of functional emphasis.

VI. 3. (b) *Situation with Respect to Other Societies.* The presence or absence of open conflict with other societies, of free trade relations or cultural diffusion, all influence the class structure to some extent. A chronic state of warfare tends to place emphasis upon the military functions, especially when the opponents are more or less equal. Free trade, on the other hand, strengthens the hand of the trader at the expense of the warrior and priest. Free movement of ideas generally has an equalitarian effect. Migration and conquest create special circumstances.

VI. 4. (c) *Size of the Society.* A small society limits the degree to which functional specialization can go, the degree of segregation of different strata, and the magnitude of inequality.

VII. Composite Types

VII. 1. Much of the literature on stratification has attempted to classify concrete systems into a certain number of types. This task is deceptively simple, however, and should come at the end of an analysis of elements and principles, rather than at the beginning. If the preceding discussion has any validity, it indicates that there are a number of modes of variation between different systems, and that any one system is a composite of the society's status with reference to all these modes of variation. The danger of trying to classify whole societies under such rubrics as *caste, feudal,* or *open class* is that one or two criteria are selected and others ignored, the result being an unsatisfactory solution to the problem posed. The present discussion has been offered as a possible approach to the more systematic classification of composite types.

Section Three

Appraising Policies

We could define *Political analysis,* as well as *social and political inquiry,* as a many-sided enterprise that embraces "testing causal theories against factual material," eliciting "principles" from factual material, interpreting "a process or institution," appraising governmental policies, and appraising "proposed reforms."[1] The tasks of appraising extant and advocated policies are generally the most difficult and controversial.

Policy decisions are commonly fraught with controversy because they involve the exercise of power. The enactment of a public policy usually means that coveted resources, such as money, are transferred from certain persons to others. Rarely are the costs and benefits distributed equally. Rarely do all persons affected feel equally gratified by the results. (We do not mean to imply that a public policy cannot bring net gains for most, or even all, persons affected.) Moreover, policy decisions breed controversy because the comparative merits of alternative allocations of resources are difficult to determine. Among other things, two distinct kinds of appraisal must be made. One has to do with matters of fact, including matters of cause and effect. As previous exercises in this volume illustrate, the causes of a given effect are often exceedingly hard to isolate. For this reason, the consequences of alternative courses of action are difficult to estimate. At the same time, policy questions involve matters of value or questions about what effects, for what persons, in what proportions, at what price, are "good" or "right."

Social scientists can contribute in a limited way to rational policy-making. As experts on a given subject, they can help to clarify, if not to settle, the questions of fact. They cannot, as professionals, resolve the questions of value. They cannot

---

[1] R. E. Lane, J. D. Barber, and F. I. Greenstein, *An Introduction to Political Analysis* (Englewood Cliffs, N.J.: Prentice-Hall, 1962), p. iii.

assert authoritatively that condition x is preferable to condition y or that policy p, because it assuredly fosters condition x, ought to be enacted.[2]

Certain conventions about the tasks of advocates reflect the two kinds of appraisal that must be made of the merits of alternative policies. The exponent of innovation in public policy bears a double burden of proof. He must first persuade us of the existence of an unmet need—that something we deem valuable is currently in unnecessarily short supply or in jeopardy. Then he must convince us that the course of action he advocates will best meet this need.

As listeners and as potential policy-choosers, we must constantly ask whether the need has been established and whether a workable solution has been proposed. These questions recur as rival advocates unfold their respective *lines* of argument. Each line of argument is an alleged reason for adopting a specified course of action. Each involves, implicitly or explicitly, a proposed *standard* for evaluating results, as well as an effort (or at least an obligation) to establish that an allegedly desirable result will indeed flow from the proposed course of action. In appraising a line of argument, accordingly, you should bear in mind two basic questions: Is it relevant? Is it plausible?

In assessing relevance, you should decide what ends, in what order of priority, you feel are worthy of achieving or augmenting. Your decisions in this realm cannot be deemed right or wrong. They *can be* more or less clear and more or less conventional. You would be confused, for example, if you could not derive a practical conclusion about what ought to be done from the assumption that United States withdrawal from the United Nations would increase the likelihood of global nuclear war. You would be eccentric and misanthropic if you invoked this assumption on behalf of the practical conclusion that the United States *should* withdraw from the United Nations.

In assessing the plausibility of a line of argument about policy, you should judge the truth of a claim about cause and effect. Your decisions in this realm cannot, again, be deemed right or wrong. But they can be deemed more or less sophisticated. You would deserve low marks for sophistication, for example, if you regarded the assertion that United States withdrawal from the United Nations would augment the likelihood of nuclear holocaust as a *self-evident* truth. Just what would constitute conclusive proof of such a proposition is indeed difficult to say. However, some general principles for assessing plausibility have been devised over the years, and you are likely to discover some of these as you work through the following exercises.

---

[2] However, social scientists can shed some light on disputes over values. They can help us when some of our values are instrumental in our minds and others are terminal. An instrumental value, in essence, is a dual belief that some x is good because it favors (protects, promotes) some y, which also is good. A social scientist might have information indicating that x actually imperils y. To that extent he can show us that our esteem for x is misplaced—is irrational. For example, the rent control law in New York City was passed for the purpose, as its sponsors avow, of preserving moderate-income rental housing. The law evidently has had the effect of virtually eliminating such housing, while providing a public subsidy for the living costs of upper-income renters. See G. Sternlieb, "New York's Housing," *The Public Interest,* Summer 1969, pp. 123–138, esp. footnote 2.

Exercise 26. Equity and Wage–Price Guideposts

In 1962 President Kennedy urged that wage rate increases in the United States be held within a limit of 3.2 percent, an amount equaling the estimated current rate of increase in labor productivity. According to economist Paul Samuelson, a number of financial columnists and corporation executives protested against this approach to a suggested ceiling, basing their protests on "arithmetical falsity." They assumed that if labor productivity grows by 3.2 percent and wages rise by the same percentage, then zero percent of the fruits of technological progress to go to profit is left over. And yet much, probably most, improvement in labor productivity, they argued, is attributable to better tools, better management methods, and improved scientific know-how.

Samuelson agreed that it would indeed be "unfair and unworkable" if "all the fruits of progress were to go to labor alone." But "critics who use this argument," he added, "have failed in their elementary arithmetic. The truth is that a 3 percent increase in labor productivity matched by a 3 percent increase in wages entails exactly a _____ percent increase in profits. To clinch this, suppose we begin with 700 of wages and 300 of profit, or 1,000 in all. Let productivity grow by 3 percent so that we now have _____ to divide. A 3 percent increase in wages does not use up the whole of the extra _____, but rather [uses up] _____, with _____ left over for profit. But what is this _____? It is exactly _____ times profit's original [sum of] _____."

Your assignment is (1) to fill in the numbers that have been left blank and (2) to state in words what Samuelson was getting at. (You may find it convenient to fill in the first blank after you have filled in the others.)

Exercise 27. Should Conventional A–B–C–D–F Grading Be Abandoned?

Evaluation of students' academic performance has long been a sore subject. The task usually bothers instructors, and the results often concern students. Until recently, arguments about evaluation were addressed primarily to the accuracy and the equity of alternative methods: What sort of scoring system should be used to evaluate what sorts of things by what persons. But, the controversy has recently reached a new level. In January 1970, for example, Jack Sawyer of Northwestern University announced that every student enrolled in his Social Conflict course would "receive an A, regardless of 'performance,' class attendance or anything else. There are no required papers, exams, reports, etc." He thus raised, and in effect answered, a question about the propriety of evaluation itself, or at least of evaluation by instructors rather than by students.

This episode followed by several months the publication of an essay, "Why Are There Grades?", in the undergraduate newspaper at the University of Chicago.

Your assignment is to examine that essay, critically, concisely, and constructively. In so doing, bear in mind these questions: What does the author advocate? What standards does he use for assessing present arrangements and for evaluating alternatives? Are these standards "appropriate" to the case? Are they exhaustive or are additional tests of merit applicable? What evidence about cause and effect does the author adduce? Is the evidence relevant? Is it sufficient? Does it do the work the author claims? What lines of argument and what kinds of evidence are conspicuous by their absence?

Incidentally, after you have dissected the essay, you should have a better understanding of the term *sophomoric*.

Ed Birnbaum

Why Are There Grades?

1. "Why are there grades?" you may ask.
2. One student, while brooding over his exams, could only conclude that they were either willed by God during his seven-day burst of creativity or were part of a profit-making conspiracy by the "blue-book" industry.
3. For who else profits by the system which establishes, as the measure of a complicated process of personal development, the achievement of a simple symbol of good performance during a competitive trial of doubtful validity? This system is not universally adhered to in the rest of the world, by all American colleges, or even by all professors here at Chicago. However, it is imposed upon most students here and some of the results were made clear last year in a study of Chicago students by William G. Spady in a dissertation for our Department of Education.
4. He found that concern over grades was a major source of depression for students of both sexes and the greatest single factor inducing men to leave the University. Even though a fellow might feel that he was making satisfactory intellectual development, supposedly the primary goal of study here, practical consideration of grades and depression would often cause him to leave. These results were substantiated by a student–faculty committee of grading.
5. It must be obvious, however, that grades were not instituted to make students happy. Rejecting both the theological and the Marxist analyses mentioned above, one can find four functions for some sort of evaluation of academic study. One is to provide a means for graduate schools and potential employers to assess the value to them of college graduates. Another is to communicate a student's progress to his instructors and others in the college so that they can better understand how to treat him. The student also needs an assessment of his own development. And, finally, evaluation can serve as reward and punishment and hence motivation to study.
6. Considerable evidence has been gathered to show that A–F grading is an inferior means of performing all those functions and that it might even be a barrier to intellectual development.
7. An examination of studies correlating collegiate grading and "adult achieve-

ment" in professional occupations concludes that the level of adult achievement is not predicted by letter-grade performance. There is a high correlation only between grade-attainment in college and grade attainment in graduate school. Other studies also show a wide disparity among schools in the way they distribute high and low grades, making the assessment of grade-point averages received from different schools a very tricky business.

8. As a means of communicating intellectual development to the student and to his instructor, A–F grading is inadequate and full of distortions. To begin with, it can only measure a specific kind of performance, usually on a two-hour exam. It is doubtful that performance on any such exam can ever be a good indicator of intellectual development except in certain areas of math and physics, where speed and accuracy are important criteria of academic progress.

9. Furthermore, the only examinations ever "scientifically" designed to test intellectual development in a particular area were the old comprehensives, now rarely used. In any case, present examinations test, in addition to learning, endurance, short-term retention of details, health (both physical and mental), sensitivity to the examiner's viewpoint, all of the above, or none of the above. Can a single letter grade, then, really tell very much about a student's achievement?

10. Even more serious, unless an instructor knows a student very well, he cannot know how well a student has progressed but only how he compares with other students. Thus, a student who has actually made considerable progress during a year might only be told by his instructor that his exam was worth a C, 23rd in the class, information which is of no educational value to him and which is only likely to discourage him.

11. The most controversial aspect of grading is its usefulness as a goad to academic work. There will probably be disagreement among psychologists about motivation during the lifetime of this writer. However, we do have evidence that grading does not provide sufficient motivation to do useful academic work for all students.

12. In one study, Professors Pauline Sears and Ernest Hilgard found that "low-anxious" students did better on a laboratory task than "high-anxious" students and that pressure to complete the task improve performance for the former, but not for the latter. This study sheds light both on the low reliability of competitive examinations and on their limited ability to provide motivation.

13. Kenneth Kenniston's famous study of particularly alienated Harvard students, "The Uncommitted," showed that these boys reacted very unfavorably to competition and to coercion. They avoided assignments in graded courses but labored impressively on intellectual projects that suited them regardless of grades. Kenniston wrote that, while the subjects of his study were rare, pure specimens, almost ideal types, they were more nearly representative of most students at Harvard than were the very committed students who played by the rules with enthusiasm.

14. All this indicates that letter grading is of doubtful value; many employers and most graduate schools, however, will probably continue to require grade-

point averages in applications for employment or admission. For them they serve as simple, superficially unambiguous means of distinguishing among their many applicants. Would-be reformers at this school thus have little control over what other institutions choose to do.

15. However, even when recognized as a necessary evil, the problem can be partially alleviated. Numerous other schools, including Princeton, Columbia, Brown, the University of Minnesota, Caltech, and others are now permitting their students to take a limited number of ungraded courses.

16. There are few reports on these recent experiments. Caltech has reported that among first-year students there has been a higher incidence of unpreparedness in class and some "disorientation" among students used to the standard means of evaluation, but also a lower drop-out rate. At our own school, some professors have been giving "P's and F's" despite their lack of formal recognition and have expressed satisfaction with the results.

17. Professor Eugene Gendlin, who has taught such courses in philosophy and psychology, said that some people did and others did not make strenuous efforts, but that such work as they did do was more "real," more meaningful, and therefore more valuable to them than if it had been forced by the threat of a low grade. Mr. Gendlin feels that in any case a given course is only successful to some proportion of the class, but that in an ungraded class, even those for whom the course is less successful seem to be launched on processes of exploration that are valuable to them.

18. Peter Rabinowitz, a graduate student and formerly an assistant instructor in liberal arts (which is graded entirely by P's and F's), said that this method "in no way tends to result in slackness. I have not once had kids come in unprepared for class." This was despite the fact that most students were simultaneously taking graded courses.

19. Professor James Redfield, master of the New Collegiate Division and also an instructor in liberal arts, told of one girl in his Liberal Arts class who devoted herself so enthusiastically to that course, that she received poor grades in her other, graded courses and was placed on academic probation.

20. A proposal by the grading committee last year would permit students to take a limited number of common-year, major, and elective courses for "P–N" (pass-no credit). A petition circulated by Student Government endorsed a more sweeping reform permitting a student to have P–N or A–F grades in any course, allowing him to adapt his method of evaluation to his own mentality and postgraduate ambitions.

21. Adoption of the latter proposal by the college would demonstrate its committment to the highest aim of higher education. The "College Announcements" for 1965–66 announced that "The College believes that the primary purpose of education is intellectual; there may be other intriguing and even useful ends, but they are secondary." If this still be true in 1968, then the College will allow students to restrict grading when it does not serve academic functions and concentrate on intellectual development.

Exercise 28. Equity in Rent Control

During World War II, housing was extremely scarce in some parts of the United States, because people flooded these localities and building materials and workers were not available. In some of these localities, public authorities imposed ceilings on what landlords could charge for rent. Rent control commissions were set up to establish the ceilings and to hear complaints from tenants and landlords. Some of these commissions outlasted the war.

In the city of Gotham, a landlord whose six-unit apartment building had been under rent control since 1942 petitioned in 1950 for permission to raise his rental charges. He based his claim on evidence allegedly indicating that his expenses had increased at a much greater rate than his receipts. He supplied the following data:

	6/30/42	6/30/50	Percent increase
Receipts	$3,956.76	$4,715.76	12
Expenses			
Janitorial	$ 363.62	$ 507.91	40
Fuel	461.96	796.05	73
Cost of ash hauling	27.00	35.00	29
Legal fees, management	96.36	189.92	97
Insurance	36.34	71.74	97
Taxes	560.03	696.99	24
			60

Your assignment is to discuss the merits of this landlord's petition. On the basis of the data, should he be granted permission to raise his rental charges? If so, by what amount and why? If not, why not? (In case you are in doubt, the assignment invites you not only to examine the landlord's raw figures but also to indicate what additional information you deem necessary as a basis for arriving at a decision in this matter.)

Exercise 29. Liberty and Slavery

No sane, reasonable, knowledgeable man, imbued with the kinds of values common in the Western world, could oppose liberty and favor slavery, right? Wrong. Some eminently sane, reasonable, knowledgeable men, professing to be Christians, antimonarchists, and exponents of material prosperity, material security, order, harmony, and progress among human beings, have in fact argued in favor of slavery.

George Fitzhugh (1806–81) was such a man. Fitzhugh belonged to the aristocratic circles of Alexandria, Virginia. He was a lawyer, a land-claim agent in the office of the Attorney General during the presidency of William Buchanan, a visiting lecturer at Harvard and Yale, a serious student of treatises on politics, economics, and sociology, and a stalwart champion of the South's Peculiar Institution. In the years before the Civil War, Fitzhugh published many articles in Southern proslavery journals. In 1854 he published *Sociology for the South; or, The Failure of Free Society*. In 1857 this volume was followed by *Cannibals All! or, Slaves Without Masters*. Unlike many of his Southern friends, Fitzhugh did not try to build his case for slavery on the foundations of a simpleminded sort of racism or on bogus Bible quoting.

Your assignment is to discuss critically and incisively the character and the merits of Fitzhugh's arguments presented in the following excerpts from *Sociology for the South*. Essentially you should try to turn Fitzhugh's lines of reasoning against his proslavery conclusion. You may be in a position to tap special information (for example, death rates among Negro slaves exceeded death rates among nonslaves, or few men indeed voluntarily opted for chattel slavery whereas many Negro slaves made desperate bids to escape their bondage); however, you should not rely primarily on such information. Nor should you allow your passions to lead you into elaborate but otherwise vague rhetorical outbursts. You will not find Fitzhugh's arguments easy to break down; but if you cannot do so, you will be confessing, in effect, that slavery really is an expedient human institution.

In preparing your critique, you may find the following questions helpful:

How does Fitzhugh define and measure slavery? If he uses more than one definition and/or way of measuring, are these compatible? What effects does he impute to slavery and to free society? Are any of the effects he imputes to slavery déplorable by your standards? In what way and to what extent does Fitzhugh's treatment depend for its persuasiveness on arbitrary assumptions about racial differentiation? How does Fitzhugh go about substantiating his claims that slavery fosters beneficial results? In the course of his maintaining that slavery is beneficial and free society is detrimental, what historical comparisons does Fitzhugh make? In other words, what *cases* does he use and how does he use them?

George Fitzhugh

The Failure of Free Society*

I. Introduction

I. 1. Society has been so quiet and contented in the [American] South — it has suffered so little from crime or extreme poverty, that its attention has not been awakened to the revolutionary tumults, uproar, mendicity, and crime of free so-

*From George Fitzhugh, *Sociology for the South; or The Failure of Free Society* (Richmond, Va., 1854), pp. iii, 7, 9–12, 29–40, 43–48, 82–87, 92, 94–95, 161–63, 169–71, 175–93. These excerpts closely follow the selections made by the Staff of Social Sciences I of the College of the University of Chicago, for *The People Shall Judge* (Chicago: University of Chicago Press, 1949), vol. 1.

ciety. Few are aware of the blessings they enjoy or of the evils from which they are exempt.

I. 2. From some peculiarity of taste, we have for many years been watching closely the perturbed workings of free society. Its crimes, its revolutions, its sufferings, and its beggary have led us to investigate its past history as well as to speculate on its future destiny. . . .

II. Free Trade

II. 1. Political economy is the science of free society. Its theory and its history alike establish this position. Its fundamental maxims, *laissez faire* and *pas trop gouverner* [roughly, "leave alone" and "not too much government"], are at war with all kinds of slavery, for they in fact assert that individuals and peoples prosper most when governed least. . . .

II. 2. Until [recently], industry had been controlled and directed by a few minds. Monopoly in its every form had been rife. Men were suddenly called on to walk alone, to act and work for themselves without guide, advice, or control from superior authority. In the past, nothing like it had occurred; hence no assistance could be derived from books. The prophets themselves had overlooked or omitted to tell of the advent of this golden era and were no better guides than the historians and philosophers. A philosophy that should guide and direct industry was equally needed with a philosophy of morals. The occasion found and made the man. For writing a one-sided philosophy, no man was better fitted than Adam Smith. He possessed extraordinary powers of abstraction, analysis, and generalization. He was absent, secluded, and unobservant. . . .

II. 3. Adam Smith's philosophy is simple and comprehensive (*teres et rotundus*). Its leading and almost its only doctrine is that individual well-being and social and national wealth and prosperity will be best promoted by each man's eagerly pursuing his own selfish welfare unfettered and unrestricted by legal regulations, or governmental prohibitions, further than such regulations may be necessary to prevent positive crime. That some qualifications of this doctrine will be found in his book we will not deny; but this is his system. It is obvious enough that such a governmental policy as this doctrine would result in would stimulate energy, excite invention and industry, and bring into livelier action genius, skill, and talent. . . . . [Smith's] friends and acquaintances were of that class who, in the war of the wits to which free competition invited, were sure to come off victors. His country too, England and Scotland, in the arts of trade and in manufacturing skill, was an overmatch for the rest of the world. International free trade would benefit his country as much as social free trade would benefit his friends. This was his world, and had it been the only world his philosophy would have been true. . . .

II. 4. A maxim well calculated not only to retard the progress of civilization but to occasion its retrogression has grown out of the science of political economy. "The world is too much governed" has become quite an axiom with many politicians. Now the need of law and government is just in proportion to man's wealth and enlightenment. Barbarians and savages need and will submit to but few and simple laws and little of government. The love of personal liberty and freedom from all restraint are distinguishing traits of wild men and wild beasts. Our Anglo-Saxon ancestors loved personal liberty because they were barbarians, but they did not love it half so much as North American Indians or Bengal tigers, because they were not half so savage. As civilization advances, liberty recedes; and it is fortunate for man that he loses his love of liberty just as fast as he becomes more moral and intellectual. The wealthy, virtuous, and religious citizens of large towns enjoy less of liberty than any other persons whatever, and yet they are the most useful and rationally happy of all mankind. The best-governed countries, and those which have prospered most, have always been distinguished for the number and stringency of their laws. Good men obey superior authority, the laws of God, of mortality, and of their country; bad men love liberty and violate them. It would be difficult very often for the most ingenious casuist to distinguish between sin and liberty, for virtue consists in the performance of duty and the obedience to that law or power that imposes duty, whilst sin is but the violation of duty and disobedience to such law and power. It is remarkable, in this connection, that sin began by the desire for liberty and the attempt to attain it in the person of Satan and his fallen angels.

II. 5. The world wants good government and a plenty of it—not liberty. It is deceptive in us to boast of our democracy, to assert the capacity of the people for self-government, and then refuse to them its exercise. In New England, and in all our large cities, where the people govern most, they are governed best. If government be not too much centralized, there is little danger of too much government. The danger and evil with us is of too little. Carlyle says of our institutions that they are "anarchy plus a street constable." We ought not to be bandaged up too closely in our infancy; it might prevent growth and development; but the time is coming when we shall need more of government if we would secure the permanency of our institutions.

II. 6. All men concur in the opinion that some government is necessary. Even the political economist would punish murder, theft, robbery, gross swindling, etc.; but they encourage men to compete with and slowly undermine and destroy one another by means quite as effective as those they forbid. We have heard a distinguished member of this school object to Negro slavery, because the protection it afforded to an inferior race would perpetuate that race, which, if left free to compete with the whites, must be starved out in a few generations. Members of Congress, of the Young American party, boast that the Anglo-Saxon race is manifestly destined to eat out all other races, as the wire-grass destroys and takes the place of other grasses. Nay, they allege this competitive process is going on throughout all nature; the [strong] are everywhere devouring the [weak]; the hardier plants and animals destroying the weaker, and the superior races of men exterminating the inferior. They [invite] admiration for this war of nature, by which they say Providence is perfecting its own work—getting rid of what is weak and indifferent and preserving only what is strong and hardy. We see the war but not the improvement. This competitive, destructive system has been going on from the earliest records of history; and yet the plants, the animals and the men of today are not superior to those of four thousand years ago. To restrict this destructive, competitive propensity, man was endowed with reason and enabled to pass laws to protect the weak against the strong. To encourage it is to encourage the strong to oppress the weak and to violate the primary object of all government. It is strange it should have entered the head of any philosopher to set the weak, who are the majority of mankind, to competing, contending, and fighting with the strong in order to improve their condition.

II. 7. Hobbes maintains that "a state of nature is a state of war." This is untrue of a state of nature, because men are naturally associative; but it is true of a civilized state of universal liberty and free competition, such as Hobbes saw around him, and which no doubt suggested his theory. The wants of man and his history alike prove that slavery has always been part of his social organization. A less degree of subjection is inadequate for the government and protection of great numbers of human beings.

II. 8. An intelligent English writer, describing society as he saw it, uses this language:

> There is no disguising from the cool eye of philosophy, that all living creatures exist in a state of natural warfare; and that man (in hostility with all) is at enmity also with his own species; man is the natural enemy of man; and society, unable to change his nature, succeeds but in establishing a hollow truce by which fraud is substituted for violence.

II. 9. Such is free society, fairly portrayed; such are the infidel doctrines of political economy when candidly avowed. Slavery and Christianity bring about a lasting peace, not "a hollow truce." But we mount a step higher. We deny that there is a society in free countries. They who act each for himself, who are hostile, antagonistic, and competitive, are not social and do not constitute a society. We use the term "free society" for want of a better; but, like the term "free government," it is an absurdity: those who are governed are not free—those who are free are not social.

III. Failure of Free Society and Rise of Socialism

III. 1. The phenomena presented by the vassals and villeins of Europe after their liberation were the opposite of those exhibited by the wealthy and powerful classes. Pauperism and beggary, we are informed by English historians, were unknown till the villeins began to escape from their masters and attempted to practice a predatory and nomadic liberty. A liberty, we should infer from the descriptions we can get of it, very much like that of domestic animals that have gone wild — the difference in favor of the animals being that nature had made provision for them but had made none for the villeins. The new freemen were bands of thieves and beggars, infesting the country and disturbing its peace. Their physical condition was worse than when under the rule of the barons, their masters, and their moral condition worse also, for liberty had made them from necessity thieves and murderers. It was necessary to retain them in slavery, not only to support and sustain them and to prevent general mendicity, but equally necessary in order to govern them and prevent crime. The advocates of universal liberty concede that the laboring class enjoy more material comfort, are better fed, clothed, and housed as slaves than as freemen. The statistics of crime demonstrate that the moral superiority of the slave over the free laborer is still greater than his superiority in animal well-being. There never can be among slaves a class so degraded as is found about the wharves and suburbs of cities. The master requires and enforces ordinary morality and industry. We very much fear, if it were possible to indite a faithful comparison of the conduct and comfort of our free Negroes with that of the runaway Anglo-Saxon serfs, that it would be found that the Negroes have fared better and committed much less crime than the whites. But those days, the fourteenth and fifteenth centuries, were the halcyon days of vagabond liberty. The few that had escaped from bondage found a wide field and plenty of subjects for the practice of theft and mendicity. There was no law and no police adequate to restrain them, for until then their masters had kept them in order better than laws ever can. But those glorious old times have long since passed. A bloody code, a standing army, and efficient police keep them quiet enough now. Their numbers have multiplied a hundred fold, but their poverty has increased faster than their numbers. Instead of stealing and begging, and living idly in the open air, they work fourteen hours a day, cooped up in close rooms, with foul air, foul water, and insufficient and filthy food, and often sleep at night crowded in cellars or in garrets, without regard to sex. . . . How slavery could degrade men lower than universal liberty has done, it is hard to conceive; how it did and would again preserve them from such degradation is well explained by those who are loudest in its abuse. A consciousness of security, a full comprehension of his position, and a confidence in that position, and the absence of all corroding cares and anxieties, make the slave easy and self-assured in his address, cheerful, happy, and contented, free from jealousy, malignity, and envy, and at peace with all around him. His attachment to his master begets the sentiment of loyalty than which none more purifies and elevates human nature. . . .

III. 2.   The free laborer rarely has a house and home of his own; he is insecure of employment; sickness may overtake him at any time and deprive him of the means of support; old age is certain to overtake him, if he lives, and generally finds him without the means of subsistence; his family is probably increasing in numbers and is helpless and burdensome to him. In all this there is little to incite to virtue, much to tempt to crime, nothing to afford happiness, but quite enough to inflict misery. Man must be more than human to acquire a pure and a high morality under such circumstances.

III. 3. In free society the sentiments, principles, feelings, and affections of high and low, rich and poor, are equally blunted and debased by the continual war of competition. It begets rivalries, jealousies, and hatred on all hands. The poor can neither love nor respect the rich, who, instead of aiding and protecting them, are endeavoring to cheapen their labor and take away their means of subsistence. The rich can hardly respect themselves, when they reflect that wealth is the result of avarice, caution, circumspection, and hard dealing. These are the virtues which free society in its regular operation brings forth. Its moral influence is therefore no better on the rich than on the poor. The number of laborers being excessive in all old countries, they are continually struggling with, scandalizing, and underbidding each other to get places and employment. Every circumstance in the poor man's situation in free society is one of harassing care, of grievous temptation, and of excitement to anger, envy, jealousy, and malignity. That so many of the poor should nevertheless be good and pure, kind, happy, and high-minded is proof enough that the poor class is not the worst class in society. But the rich have their temptations, too. Capital gives them the power to oppress; selfishness offers the inducement, and political economy, the moral guide of the day, would justify the oppression. Yet there are thousands of noble and generous and disinterested men in free society who employ their wealth to relieve and not to oppress the poor. Still, these are exceptions to the general rule. The effect of such society is to encourage the oppression of the poor.

III. 4. The ink was hardly dry with which Adam Smith wrote his *Wealth of Nations,* lauding the benign influences of free society, ere the hunger and want and nakedness of that society engendered a revolutionary explosion that shook the world to its center. The starving artisans and laborers, and fishwomen and needlewomen of Paris, were the authors of the first French revolution, and that revolution was everywhere welcomed and spread from nation to nation like fire in the prairies. The French armies met with but a formal opposition until they reached Russia. There, men had homes and houses and a country to fight for. The serfs of Russia, the undisciplined Cossacks, fought for lares and penates, their homes, their country, and their God, and annihilated an army more numerous than that of Xerxes and braver and better appointed than the tenth legion of Caesar. What should western European poor men fight for? All the world was the same to them. They had been set free to starve, without a place to rest their dying heads or to inter their dead bodies. Any change they thought would be for the better, and hailed Bonaparte as a deliverer. . . .

III. 5. The Chartists and Radicals of England would in some way subvert and reconstruct society. They complain of free competition as a crying evil and may be classed with the Socialists. The high conservative party called Young England vainly endeavors, by preaching fine sentiments, to produce that good feeling between the rich and the poor, the weak and the powerful, which slavery alone can bring about. Liberty places those classes in positions of antagonism and war. Slavery identifies the interests of rich and poor, master and slave, and begets domestic affection on the one side, and loyalty and respect on the other. Young England [a political group] sees clearly enough the character of the disease but is not bold enough to propose an adequate remedy. The poor themselves are all practical Socialists and in some degree proslavery men. They unite in strikes and trades-unions and thus exchange a part of their liberties in order to secure high and uniform wages. The exchange is a prudent and sensible one; but they who have bartered off liberty are fast verging toward slavery. Slavery to an association is not always better than slavery to a single master. The professed object is to avoid ruinous underbidding and competition with one another; but this competition can never cease whilst liberty lasts. Those who wish to be free must take liberty with this inseparable burden. Old-Fellows' societies, temperance societies, and all other societies that provide for sick and unfortunate members are instances of socialism. The muse in England for many years has been busy in composing dissonant laborer songs, bewailing the hardships, penury, and sufferings of the poor, and indignantly rebuking the cruelty and injustice of their hard-hearted and close-fisted employers.

III. 6. Dickens and Bulwer denounce the framework of society quite as loudly as Carlyle and Newman; the two latter of whom propose slavery as a remedy for existing evils. A large portion of the clergy are professed Socialists, and there is scarcely a literary man in England who is not ready to propose radical and organic changes in her social system. Germany is full of Communists; social discontent is universal, and her people are leaving en masse for America—hopeless of any amelioration at home for the future. Strange to tell, in the free states of America too, socialism and every other heresy that can be invoked to make war on existing institutions prevail to an alarming extent. Even according to our own theory of the necessity of slavery, we should not suppose that that necessity would be so soon felt in a new and sparsely settled country, where the supply of labor does not exceed the demand. But it is probable the constant arrival of emigrants makes the situation of the laborer at the North as precarious as in Europe and produces a desire for some change that shall secure him employment and support at all times. Slavery alone can effect that change; and toward slavery the North and all western Europe are unconsciously marching. The master-evil they all complain of is free competition—which is another name for liberty. Let them remove that evil, and they will find themselves slaves, with all the advantages and disadvantages of slavery. They will have attained association of labor, for slavery produces association of labor and is one of the ends all Communists and Socialists desire. A well-conducted farm in the South is a model of associated labor that Fourier might envy. One old woman nurses all the children whilst the mothers are at work; another waits on the sick, in a house set aside for them. Another washes and cooks, and a fourth makes and mends the clothing. It is a great economy of labor and is a good idea of the Socialists.

III. 7. Slavery protects the infants, the aged, and the sick; nay, takes far better care of them than of the healthy, the middle-aged, and the strong. They are part of the family, and self-interest and domestic affection combine to shelter, shield, and foster them. A man loves not only his horses and his cattle, which are useful to him, but he loves his dog, which is of no use. He loves them because they are his. What a wise and beneficent provision of Heaven that makes the selfishness of man's nature a protecting aegis to shield and defend wife and children, slaves and even dumb animals. The Socialists propose to reach this result too, but they never can if they refuse to march in the only road Providence has pointed out. Who will check, govern, and control their superintending authority? Who prevent his abuse of power? Who can make him kind, tender, and affectionate to the poor, aged, helpless, sick, and unfortunate? *Qui custodiat custodes?* Nature establishes the only safe and reliable checks and balances in government. Alton Locke describes an English farm, where the cattle, the horses, and the sheep are fat, plentifully fed, and warmly housed; the game in the preserves and the fish in the pond carefully provided for; and two freezing, shivering, starving, half-clad boys, who have to work on the Sabbath, are the slaves to these animals and are vainly endeavoring to prepare their food. Now it must have occurred to the author that if the boys had belonged to the owner of the farm, they too would have been well treated, happy, and contented. This farm is but a miniature of all England; every animal is well treated and provided for, except the laboring man. He is the slave of the brutes, the slave of society, produces everything and enjoys nothing. Make him the slave of one man instead of the slave of society, and he would be far better off. None but lawyers and historians are aware how much of truth, justice, and good sense there is in the notions of the Communists as to the community of property. Laying no stress on the too abstract proposition that Providence gave the world not to one man, or set of men, but to all mankind, it is a fact that all governments, in civilized countries, recognize the obligation to support the poor and thus, in some degree, make all property a common possession. The poor-laws and poor-houses of England are founded on communistic principles. Each parish is compelled to support its own poor. In Ireland this obligation weighs so heavily as in many instances to make farms valueless, the poor rates exceeding the rents. But it is domestic slavery alone that can establish a safe, efficient, and humane community of property. It did so in ancient times; it did so in feudal times; and does so now, in eastern Europe, Asia, and America. Slaves never die of hunger, seldom suffer want. Hence Chinese sell themselves when they can do no better. A southern farm is a sort of joint stock concern, or social phala[n]stery, in which the master furnishes the capital and skill, and the slaves the labor, and divide the profits, not according to each one's input, but according to each one's wants and necessities.

III. 8. Socialism proposes to do away with free competition; to afford protection and support at all times to the laboring class; to bring about, at least, a qualified community of property and to associate labor. All these purposes slavery fully and perfectly attains. . . .

IV. Negro Slavery

IV. 1. ... Now, it is clear the Athenian democracy would not suit a Negro nation, nor will the government of mere law suffice for the individual Negro. He is but a grown-up child and must be governed as a child, not as a lunatic or criminal. The master occupies toward him the place of parent or guardian. We shall not dwell on this view, for no one will differ with us who thinks as we do of the Negro's capacity, and we might argue till doomsday, in vain, with those who have a high opinion of the Negro's moral and intellectual capacity.

IV. 2. Secondly, the Negro is improvident; will not lay up in summer for the wants of winter; will not accumulate in youth for the exigencies of age. He would become an insufferable burden to society. Society has the right to prevent this and can only do so by subjecting him to domestic slavery.

IV. 3. In the last place, the Negro race is inferior to the white race, and, living in their midst, they would be far outstripped or outwitted in the chase of free competition. Gradual but certain extermination would be their fate. We presume the maddest abolitionist does not think the Negro's providence of habits and money-making capacity at all to compare to those of the whites. This defect of character would alone justify enslaving him, if he is to remain here. In Africa or the West Indies, he would become idolatrous, savage, and cannibal, or be devoured by savages and cannibals. At the North he would freeze or starve.

IV. 4. We would remind those who deprecate and sympathize with Negro slavery that his slavery here relieves him from a far more cruel slavery in Africa, or from idolatry and cannibalism, and every brutal vice and crime that can disgrace humanity; and that it Christianizes, protects, supports, and civilizes him; that it governs him far better than free laborers at the North are governed. ...

IV. 5. But abolish Negro slavery, and how much of slavery still remains. Soldiers and sailors in Europe enlist for life; here, for five years. Are they not slaves who have not only sold their liberties but their lives also? And they are worse treated than domestic slaves. No domestic affection and self-interest extend their aegis over them. No kind mistress, like a guardian angel, provides for them in health, tends them in sickness, and soothes their dying pillow. Wellington at Waterloo was a slave. He was bound to obey, or would, like Admiral Byng, have been shot for gross misconduct and might not, like a common laborer, quit his work at any moment. He had sold his liberty and might not regisn without the consent of his master, the king. The common laborer may quit his work at any moment, whatever his contract; declare that liberty is an inalienable right and leave his employer to redress by a useless suit for damages. The highest and most honorable position on earth was that of the slave Wellington; the lowest, that of the free man who cleaned his boots and fed his hounds. The African cannibal, caught, Christianized, and enslaved, is as much elevated by slavery as was Wellington. The kind of slavery is adapted to the men enslaved. Wives and apprentices are slaves; not in theory only but often in fact. Children are slaves to their parents, guardians, and teachers. Imprisoned culprits are slaves. Lunatics and idiots are slaves also. Three-fourths of free society are slaves, no better treated, when their wants and capacities are estimated, than Negro slaves. The masters in free society, or slave society, if they perform properly their duties, have more cares and less liberty than the slaves themselves. "In the sweat of thy face shalt thou earn thy bread!" made all men slaves, and such all *good men* continue to be.

IV. 6. Negro slavery would be changed immediately to some form of peonage, serfdom, or villeinage if the Negroes were sufficiently intelligent and provident to manage a farm. No one would have the labor and trouble of management if his Negroes would pay in hires and rents one-half what free tenants pay in rent in Europe. Every Negro in the South would be soon liberated if he would take liberty on the terms that white tenants hold it. The fact that he cannot enjoy liberty on such terms seems conclusive that he is only fit to be a slave.

IV. 7. But for the assaults of the abolitionists, much would have been done ere this to regulate and improve southern slavery. Our Negro mechanics do not work so hard, have many more privileges and holidays, and are better fed and clothed than field hands and are yet more valuable to their masters. The slaves of the South are cheated of their rights by the purchase of northern manufactures which they could produce. Besides, if we would employ our slaves in the coarser processes of the mechanic arts and manufactures, such as brick-making, getting and hewing timber for ships and houses, iron-mining and smelting, coal-mining, grading railroads and plank roads, in the manufacture of cotton, tobacco, etc., we would find a vent in new employments for their increase more humane and more profitable than the vent afforded by new states and territories. The nice and finishing processes of manufactures and mechanics should be reserved for the whites, who only are fitted for them, and thus, by diversifying pursuits and cutting off dependence on the North, we might benefit and advance the interests of our whole population. Exclusive agriculture has depressed and impoverished the South. We will not here dilate on this topic, because we intend to make it the subject of a separate essay. Free-trade doctrines, not slavery, have made the South agricultural and dependent, given her a sparse and ignorant population, ruined her cities, and expelled her people. . . .

IV. 8. But far the worst feature of modern civilization, which is the civilization of free society, remains to be exposed. Whilst labor-saving processes have probably lessened by one-half, in the last century, the amount of work needed for comfortable support, the free laborer is compelled by capital and competition to work more than he ever did before and is less comfortable. The organization of society cheats him of his earnings, and those earnings go to swell the vulgar pomp and pageantry of the ignorant millionaires, who are the only great of the present day. These reflections might seem, at first view, to have little connection with Negro slavery; but it is well for us of the South not to be deceived by the tinsel glare and glitter of free society and to employ ourselves in doing our duty at home and studying the past rather than in insidious rivalry of the expensive pleasures and pursuits of men whose sentiments and whose aims are low, sensual, and groveling. . . .

IV. 9. We deem this peculiar question of Negro slavery of very little importance. The issue is made throughout the world on the general subject of slavery in the abstract. The argument has commenced. One set of ideas will govern and control after awhile the civilized world. Slavery will everywhere be abolished or everywhere be reinstituted. We think the opponents of practical, existing slavery are estopped by their own admission; nay, that unconsciously, as Socialists, they are the defenders and propagandists of slavery and have furnished the only sound arguments on which its defense and justification can be rested. We have introduced the subject of Negro slavery to afford us a better opportunity to disclaim the purpose of reducing the white man anywhere to the condition of Negro slaves here. It would be very unwise and unscientific to govern white men as you would Negroes. Every shade and variety of slavery has existed in the world. In some cases there has been much of legal regulation, much restraint of the master's authority; in others, none at all. The character of slavery necessary to protect the whites in Europe should be much milder than Negro slavery, for slavery is only needed to protect the white man, whilst it is more necessary for the government of the Negro even than for his protection. But even Negro slavery should not be outlawed. We might and should have laws in Virginia, as in Louisiana, to make the master subject to presentment by the grand jury and to punishment for any inhuman or improper treatment or neglect of his slave.

IV. 10. We abhor the doctrine of the "Types of Mankind"; first, because it is at war with scripture, which teaches us that the whole human race is descended from a common parentage; and, secondly, because it encourages and incites brutal masters to treat Negroes, not as weak, ignorant, and dependent brethern, but as wicked beasts, without the pale of humanity. The southerner is the Negro's friend, his only friend. Let no intermeddling Abolitionist, no refined philosophy, dissolve this friendship. . . .

V. The Association of Labor

V. 1. If the Socialists had done no other good, they would be entitled to the gratitude of mankind for displaying in a strong light the advantages of the association of labor. Adam Smith, in his elaborate treatise on the "Division of Labor," nearly stumbled on the same truth. But the division of labor is a curse to the laborer, without the association of labor. Division makes labor ten times more efficient, but, by confining each workman to some simple, monotonous employment, it makes him a mere automaton and an easy prey to the capitalist. The association of labor, like all association, requires a head or ruler, and that head or ruler will become a cheat and a tyrant unless his interests are identified with the interests of the laborer. In a large factory, in free society, there is division of labor, and association too, but association and division for the benefit of the employer and to the detriment of the laborer. On a large farm whatever advances the health, happiness, and morals of the Negroes renders them more prolific and valuable to their master. It is his interest to pay them high wages in way of support, and he can afford to do so, because association renders the labor of each slave five times as productive and efficient as it would be were the slaves working separately.

V. 2. One man could not inclose an acre of land, cultivate it, send his crops to market, do his own cooking, washing, and mending. One man may live as a prowling beast of prey but not as a civilized being. One hundred human beings, men, women, and children, associated, will cultivate ten acres of land each, inclose it, and carry on every other operation of civilized life. Labor becomes at least twenty times as productive when a hundred associate as when one acts alone. The same is as true in other pursuits as in farming. But in free society the employer robs the laborer, and he is no better off than the prowling savage, although he might live in splendor if he got a fair proportion of the proceeds of his own labor.

V. 3. We have endeavored to show, heretofore, that the Negro slave, considering his indolence and unskilfulness, often gets his fair share, and sometimes more than his share, of the profits of the farm and is exempted, besides, from the harassing cares and anxieties of the free laborer. Grant, however, that the Negro does not receive adequate wages from his master, yet all admit that in the aggregate the Negroes get better wages than free laborers; therefore, it follows that, with all its imperfections, slave society is the best form of society yet devised for the masses. When Socialists and Abolitionists, by full and fair experiments, exhibit a better, it will be time to agitate the subject of abolition.

V. 4. The industrial products of black slave labor have been far greater and more useful to mankind than those of the same amount of any other labor. In a very short period the South and Southwest have been settled, cleared, fenced in, and put in cultivation by what were, a century ago, a handful of masters and slaves. This region now feeds and clothes a great part of mankind; but free trade cheats them of the profits of their labor. In the vast amount of our industrial products, we see the advantages of association; in our comparative poverty, the evils of free trade. . . .

VI. Liberty and Free Trade

VI. 1. These are convertible terms; two names for the same thing. Statesmen, orators, and philosophers, the Tories of England, and the Whigs of America, have been laboring incessantly for more than half a century to refute the doctrine of free trade. They all and each failed to produce a single plausible argument in reply. Not one of their books or speeches survived a month. Not one ever was, or ever will be, quoted or relied on as authority to disprove the principles of political economy. The reason is obvious enough; they were all confused by words or afraid to make the proper issue. They first admitted liberty to be a good, and then attempted, but attempted in vain, to argue that free trade was an evil. The Socialists stumbled on the true issue but do not seem yet fully aware of the nature of their discovery. Liberty was the evil, liberty the disease, under which society was suffering. It must be restricted, competition be arrested, the strong be restrained from, instead of encouraged to oppress the weak—in order to restore society to a healthy state. To them we are indebted for our argument against free trade. We have extended it and explained its application. *They* demonstrated that social free trade was an evil, because it incited the rich and strong to oppress the weak, poor, and ignorant. *We* saw that the disparities of mental strength were greater between races and nations than between individuals in the same society. History spoke less equivocally as to the ruinout effects of international free trade than as to those of social free trade.

VI. 2. Events are occurring every day, especially at the North, that show that religious liberty must be restricted as well as other liberty.

VI. 3. Chinese idolaters are coming in swarms, too, to California. If they are to be permitted to practice their diabolical rights, the Negroes should be allowed to revert to the time-honored customs of their ancestors and immolate human victims to their devil deity. Mormonism is still a worse religious evil, which we have to deal with.

VI. 4. Liberty is an evil which government is intended to correct. This is the sole object of government. Taking these premises, it is easy enough to refute free trade. Admit liberty to be a good, and you leave no room to argue that free trade is an evil—because liberty is free trade.

VI. 5. With thinking men, the question can never arise: Who ought to be free? Because no one ought to be free. All government is slavery. The proper subject of investigation for philosophers and philanthropists is, "Is the existing mode of government adapted to the wants of its subjects?" No one will contend that Negroes, for instance, should roam at large in *puris naturalibus,* with the apes and tigers of Africa, and "worry and devour each other." Nor are they fitted for an Athenian democracy. What form of government short of domestic slavery will suit their wants and capacities? This is the true issue, and we direct the attention of Abolitionists to it. They are now striking wild and often hit the Bible and the marriage tie and the right of property and the duties of children to their parents and guardians harder blows than they do Negro slavery. They are mere anarchists and infidels. If they would take our advice, they would appear more respectable, do less harm, and might suggest some good. For domestic slavery, like all human institutions, has its imperfections—will always have them. Yet it is our duty to correct such as can be corrected, and we would do so, if the Abolitionists would let us alone or advise with us as friends, neighbors, and gentlemen. . . .

VII. [Human Nature, Needs, Possibilities]

VII. 1. . . . Men are not born physically, morally, or intellectually equal—some are males, some females, some from birth large, strong, and healthy, others weak, small, and sickly—some are naturally amiable, others prone to all kinds of wickednesses—some brave, others timid. These natural inequalities beget inequalities of rights. The weak in mind or body require guidance, support, and protection; they must obey and work for those who protect and guide them—they have a natural right to guardians, committees, teachers, or masters. Nature has made them slaves; all that law and government can do is to regulate, modify, and mitigate their slavery. In the absence of legally instituted slavery, the condition would be worse under that natural slavery of the weak to the strong, the foolish to the wise and cunning. The wise and virtuous, the brave, the strong in mind and body, are by nature born to command and protect, and law but follows nature in making them rulers, legislators, judges, captains, husbands, guardians, committees, and masters. The naturally depraved class, those born prone to crime, are our brethren too; they are entitled to education, to religious instruction, to all the means and appliances proper to correct their evil propensities, and all their failings; they have a right to be sent to the penitentiary—for there, if they do not reform, they cannot at least disturb society. Our feelings and our consciences teach us that nothing but necessity can justify taking human life.

VII. 2.   . . . Men are not created or born equal, and circumstances and education and association tend to increase and aggravate inequalities among them from generation to generation. Generally, the rich associate and intermarry with each other, the poor do the same; the ignorant rarely associate or intermarry with the learned; and all society shuns contact with the criminal, even to the third and fourth generations.

VII. 3.   Men are not "born entitled to equal rights"! It would be far nearer the truth to say that "some were born with saddles on their backs, and others booted and spurred to ride them"—and the riding does them good. They need the reins. the bit, and the spur. No two men are by nature exactly equal or exactly alike. No institutions can prevent the few from acquiring rule and ascendance over the many. Liberty and free competition invite and encourage the attempt of the strong to master the weak and insure their success.

VII. 4.   Life and liberty are not "inalienable"; they have been sold in all countries, and in all ages, and must be sold so long as human nature lasts. It is an inexpedient and unwise and often unmerciful restraint on a man's liberty of action to deny him the right to sell himself when starving and again to buy himself when fortune smiles. Most countries of antiquity, and some, like China at the present day, allowed such sale and purchase. The great object of government is to restrict, control, and punish man "in the pursuit of happiness." All crimes are committed in its pursuit. Under the free or competitive system, most men's happiness consists in destroying the happiness of other people. This, then, is no inalienable right.

VII. 5.   The author of the Declaration [of Independence] may have, and probably did mean, that all men were created with an equal title to property. Carry out such a doctrine, and it would subvert every government on earth.

VII. 6.   In practice, in all ages, and in all countries, men had sold their liberty either for short periods, for life, or hereditarily; that is, both their own liberty and that of their children after them. The laws of all countries have, in various forms and degrees, in all times recognized and regulated this right to *alien* or liberty. The soldiers and sailors of the revolution had aliened both liberty and life; the wives in all America had aliened their liberty; so had the apprentices and wards at the very moment [the] verbose, newborn, false, and unmeaning Preamble [to the U.S. Constitution] was written.

VII. 7. . . . We may fairly conclude that liberty is alienable; that there is a natural right to alien it, first, because the laws and institutions of all countries have recognized and regulated its alienation; and, secondly, because we cannot conceive of a civilized society, in which there were no wives, no wards, no apprentices, no sailors, and no soldiers; and none of these could there be in a country that practically carried out the doctrine that liberty is inalienable.

VII. 8. . . . If all men had been created equal, all would have been competitors, rivals, and enemies. Subordination, difference of caste and classes, difference of sex, age, and slavery beget peace and good will.

VII. 9. . . . [T]he nobility of [tsarist] Russia do not hold such despotic sway over their serfs as we do over our Negroes and [the Russian nobles] are themselves mere slaves to the emperor, whilst our slaveholders have scarcely any authority above them. [The author of the Virginia Bill of Rights, with all his equalitarian delusions, apparently "saw no objection" to such arrangements being "secured by law." He probably would have said that] a man has a *natural right* to his lands and Negroes, a natural right to what belonged to his father.

VII. 10. Property is not a natural and divine but a conventional right; it is the mere creature of society and law. In this all lawyers and publicists agree. In this country the history of property is of such recent date that the simplest and most ignorant man must know that it commenced in wrong, injustice, and violence a few generations ago and derives its only title now from the will of society through the sanction of law. Society has no right, because it is not expedient, to resume any one man's property because he abuses its possession and does not so employ it as to redound to public advantage—but if all private property, or if private property generally, were so used as to injure, instead of promote public good, then society might and ought to destroy the whole institution.

VII. 11. From these premises it follows that government, in taxing private property, should only be limited by the public good. If the tax be so heavy as to deter the owner from improving the property, then, in general, will the whole public be injured.

VII. 12. False notions of the right of property, and of the duties and liabilities of property-holders, destroy all public spirit and patriotism, cripple and injure, and prevent the growth and development of the South. . . .

VII. 13. Property is too old and well tried an institution, too much interwoven with the feelings, interests, prejudices, and affections of man, to be shaken by the speculations of philosophers. It is only its maladministration that can endanger it. So far from wishing to shake or undermine property, we would, for the public good, give it more permanence. We do not like the Western Homestead provision of forty acres,[1] because that entails on families poverty and ignorance and tends to depress civilization. We do not like the large entails of England,[2] because they beget an idle, useless, and vicious aristocracy. . . . A law entailing farms of such amount as would educate families well, without putting them above the necessity of industry and exertion, would add much to national wealth, in encouraging good and permanent improvements, and would improve national character and intelligence, by securing a class of well-educated men, attached to the soil and the country. We need not fear the mad-dog cry of aristocracy; a man with an entailed estate of five hundred acres, and a coat-of-arms to boot, would not be a very dangerous character. . . . Five hundred acres of land and thirty Negroes would suffice to educate all the younger members of the family and make useful citizens of them. Primogeniture [whereby the firstborn son is the principal heir] and entails have had this good effect in England. The younger sons have filled the professions, the church, the army, and the navy with able, ambitious men. It has furnished London and Liverpool with the best merchants in the world and made trade one of the most honorable professions.

VII. 14. It is pleasing to see the poor acquiring lands, but the pleasure is more than balanced, with all save the malicious, by seeing the rich stripped of them. Those accustomed to poverty suffer little from it. Those who have been rich are miserable when they become poor. . . .

Exercise 30. Gun Control Legislation

According to commonly accepted estimates, 40 to 50 million Americans own some two hundred million pistols, rifles, shotguns, and other firearms. In November 1963 one of these weapons, a rifle, was used in Dallas, Texas, to assassinate President John F. Kennedy. In April 1968 another was used in Memphis, Tennessee, to end the life of the Reverend Martin Luther King, Jr. In June 1968 still another of these weapons, a pistol this time, was used in Los Angeles to slay Senator Robert F. Kennedy. These tragic episodes served to renew periodic demands for stiffer public controls over the sale, ownership, possession, and use of firearms. At this writing, several proposals for stiffening federal gun control legislation were pending in the Congress.

Reactions to such proposals are sometimes strictly emotional. For example, from a few spectacular deaths or from the thousands of gun-related deaths and injuries that occur every year, we might jump to the conclusions that strict regulation is needed, that the need is more acute now than ever before, that almost any approach to regulation would mark an improvement, and that the best regulations would be those which come closest to prohibiting ownership and use of firearms by anyone. Or we might regard all such controls as an in-

---

[1] [The Homestead Act provided that individuals could win title to previously public lands, in 40-acre units, if they occupied the tracts and made improvements (clearing, fencing, house-building, and so on)—*Eds.*]

[2] [English landed estates, under the law, could not be broken up and passed on to several descendants—*Eds.*]

fringement of individual liberty and insist that all such regulation is unconstitutional (because the Second Amendment ordains that "the right of the people to keep and bear arms shall not be infringed"). Further, we might assume that if guns were outlawed, only outlaws would have guns.

The merits of gun control legislation may also be weighed rationally. We might painstakingly analyze historical changes in the supply of firearms, in rates of crime, and in the use of firearms in crimes and suicides and series accidents, as well as carefully study contrasts in firearms-related injuries in localities that differ in, among other things, the character of their public laws concerning firearms. From such studies we attempt to learn the scale of the firearms problem, the extent to which public laws affect the problem, and the kinds of regulations that more or less directly produce various results.

The following selection is an example, or what appears to be an example, of the rationalistic approach to gun control legislation. It is a slightly abridged version of a pamphlet that the National Shooting Sports Foundation of Riverside, Connecticut, published in April 1968. The pamphlet contains three studies previously published (in July 1967, January 1968, and April 1968) in the *Congressional Record*. According to the cover page of the pamphlet, legislators and newsmen heretofore have been "fed a steady diet of partial statistics, and often statistics pulled out of context," on the subject of gun control. These partial statistics allegedly have misled the public about what gun control legislation can accomplish. But relief is in sight. The new threefold study by Alan S. Krug, an economist formerly with the Institute for Research on Land and Water Resources at Pennsylvania State University, now assistant to the director of the National Shooting Sports Foundation, uses "*all* of the pertinent statistics available" and thus is "the first comprehensive study on a national basis ever made on the relationship of firearms to crime in the United States. Most of the statistics are from the Federal Bureau of Investigation."

However, according to some students of gun control legislation, "The True Facts on Firearms Legislation" really is a vivid example of partial interpretation and biased reasoning. Moreover, in the final analysis, the article allegedly fails to sustain the claim that new control legislation is superfluous.

Your assignment is to examine Krug's article critically, from the standpoint of a rationalistic believer in gun control legislation. Thus you should try to vindicate gun control legislation on the basis of material in the article, by showing that "The True Facts" fails to make the opposite case. For the purpose of the exercise, you should assume that Krug accurately cites sources of his statistics. Confine your attention to how he uses statistics.

In building your case, you may find these questions helpful:

On the basis of the data he presents, is Krug warranted in saying that from 1910 until the present time the firearm homicide rate in the United States has shown a decided downward trend?

To what extent can Krug's evidence (especially in section I) be reconciled with the inference that gun prohibitions would *reduce* major crime?

Is there internal evidence that the bulk of the so-called "trend" depicted in Table 1 of section I is due to false or faulty comparisons? to unreliable data?

To what extent and in what manner can you find fault with the statement that

"Firearms were misused in 3.4% of the 3,243,370 serious crimes that were committed in the U.S. in 1966"? Can you rationalize a substantially higher estimate, on the basis of Krug's data?

Can you negate Krug's negation of the hypothesis (in section II) that States with firearm licensing laws have lower crime rates than States without such laws?

Can you find internal evidence for doubting Krug's inference that a "negative correlation" exists between "the index of firearms ownership and serious crime, aggravated assault and robbery . . ."? Does this argument (section III) have an unsupported major premise that vitiates the inference?

Alan S. Krug

The True Facts on Firearms Legislation: Three Statistical Studies*

I. The Misuses of Firearms in Crime: Extent of the Problem

Introductory

I. 1. The need to prevent abuses in interstate firearms sales through realistic federal legislation has been recognized by the overwhelming majority of American sportsmen and other law-abiding firearms owners in the United States. All the major organizations representing these interests have endorsed proposals which are now pending before the Congress. Other groups have proposed measures which law-abiding firearms owners believe are overly restrictive and ineffective. It is generally agreed that enactment of any new firearms legislation will be realized only through mutual understanding between all interested parties. However, positive action is being blocked by the anti-gun faction's dissemination of false and misleading statistics on the subject of the misuse of firearms in crime. The use of such "doctored" material serves only to alienate those sportsmen who are familiar with the facts. By misleading much of the general public with manufactured material, the anti-gun faction contributes nothing to the constructive dialogue over firearms control. Rather, it drives the two positions farther apart.

Fact and fancy

I. 2. One very misleading statistic that has been used in a number of emotionally charged anti-firearm newspaper editorials and magazine articles is that, in 1965, 17,000 Americans were "killed by guns." While these 17,000 deaths were represented to be murders committed with firearms, the actual number of criminal homicides involving firearms in that year was 5,634. The remainder of

*Most citations have been deleted. Numbers of statistical tables have been changed.

the 17,000 people who were "killed by guns" died through suicide (8,898) and firearms accidents (2,200).

I. 3. Another statistic of anti-firearm writers is that "750,000 Americans have died since 1900 by means of firearms." Here again, the implication is that all of these people were murdered with guns. However, upon closer inspection, it is seen that this figure too includes deaths due to criminal homicide, firearms accidents and suicide. This particular statistic was originally manufactured by a New York City press agent to help sell an extremist anti-gun book. There are no reliable data available from any private or public source to substantiate it. J. Edgar Hoover, Director of the FBI, said in reference to the 750,000 "deaths" that "This Bureau does not have any reliable figures or estimates on the total number of Americans killed by firearms since 1900. We began compiling data on this subject in 1961, . . ."

I. 4. Data on the number of homicides in the United States involving firearms and explosives are available from the U.S. Department of Health, Education, and Welfare, Public Health Service, for the years 1933 to 1966. Some data are available for the period 1910 to 1932, but only for "Death-registration States," and not for the entire United States. Data for homicides by type of weapon used are not available for any years prior to 1910. In no case are the data disaggregated into deaths by firearms and deaths by explosives. A second deficiency in the data is that the homicides are not broken down into criminal homicides and justifiable homicides.

I. 5. Unfortunately, such fabricated, misleading statistics influence not only the general public but individuals who are seriously interested in the question of the misuse of firearms in crime. This is well demonstrated by the recent testimony of Attorney General Ramsey Clark before a subcommittee of the U.S. House of Representatives. Both the 17,000 and the 750,000 figures were used by Attorney General Clark, who testified in favor of the enactment of H. R. 5384, the House version of Amendment 90 to S. 1, the current "Dodd bill." He made the amazing statements in regard to the 17,000 statistic that "Actually, we are unable to make a specific breakdown (as to those deaths which were the result of criminal activity and those that were due to accidents and suicide—*Ed*.)," and "It may be that most of them (the 17,000 deaths—*Ed*.) are the result of criminal acts."

I. 6. These statements were made in spite of the fact that the number of criminal homicides involving firearms in 1965 was published by the Federal Bureau of Investigation, an agency of the U.S. Department of Justice, which Attorney General Clark heads. (Both the number of accidental deaths and suicides involving firearms were available from the U.S. Public Health Service, U.S. Department of Health, Education and Welfare. In 1965, criminal homicides involving firearms totaled 5,634, hardly "most of them.")

I. 7. When asked for a breakdown of the 750,000 figure, the attorney general said "I would assume that accidental death would be among the highest." Actually, the number of accidental deaths by firearms is the lowest of the three categories of firearms deaths as mentioned above for each of the years for which data are available.

I. 8. Thus, it can be seen that it is all too easy for statistics that have "popped up" in some popular article to be taken for scientific fact, when in truth they constitute little more than "gossip." Such situations as this represent a real threat to any attempt to present the problem of the misuse of firearms in a scientific light. The result can only be confusion, consternation and resentment on the part of those who are attempting to judge proposed firearms legislation.

Firearm homicide, 1910–1967

I. 9. From 1910 until the present time, the firearm homicide rate in the United States has shown a decidedly downward trend. This is depicted in the graph of Figure 1, which is a time series of the national firearm homicide rate [and is based on the data summarized in Table 1]. The trend line, which was fitted to the data of the time series by the method of least squares, indicates that the magnitude of the problem of the misuse of firearms in homicides has been decreasing, not increasing, over the entire period for which data are available.[1]

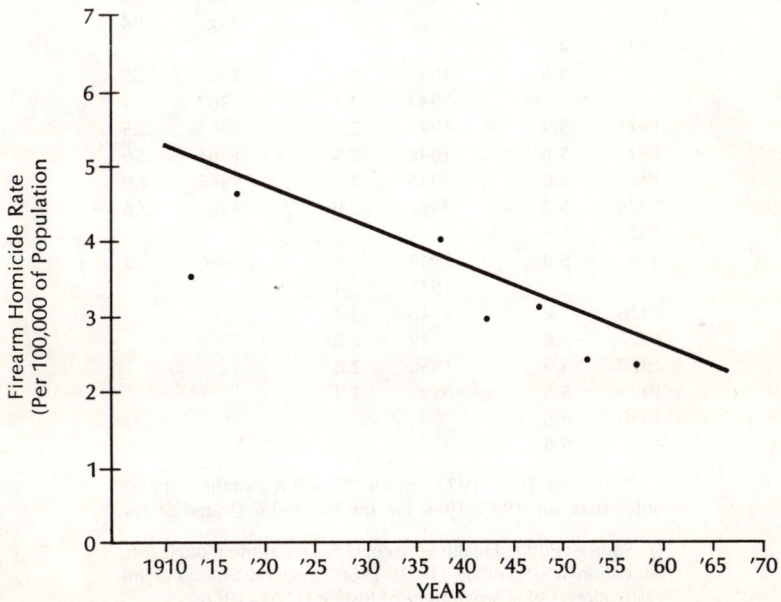

Figure 1. Trend of the firearm homicide rate in the United States: 1910–1966.*

*Data for 1910–1932 are for "Death-registration States" only; data for 1933–1966 are for the entire United States. The trend line was constructed from the annual data for the period 1910–1966. The dots represent the average firearm homicide rate for each five-year period 1911–1965. See Table 1.

[1] A *time series* is a series of successive observations of the same phenomenon over a period of time. A trend line represents that characteristic of a time series, which extends consistently throughout the entire period of time under consideration. For explanation of "the method of least squares," see W. J. Dixon and F. J. Massey, Jr., *Introduction to Statistical Analysis* (New York: McGraw-Hill Book Co., 1957), 189–93 [from Krug's footnotes—Ed.].

Table 1. Firearm homicide rates in the United States: 1910–1966.*

Year	Rate	Year	Rate	Year	Rate
1910	2.5	1931	6.2	1951	2.5
		1932	6.1	1952	2.7
1911	3.2	1933	6.3	1953	2.5
1912	3.2	1934	6.1	1954	2.5
1913	3.6	1935	5.1	1955	2.3
1914	3.9	Avg.	6.0	Avg.	2.5
1915	3.6				
Avg.	3.5	1936	4.7	1956	2.4
		1937	4.4	1957	2.3
1916	4.0	1938	3.9	1958	2.4
1917	4.6	1939	3.7	1959	2.5
1918	4.4	1940	3.5	1960	2.6
1919	5.1	Avg.	4.0	Avg.	2.4
1920	4.8				
Avg.	4.6	1941	3.4	1961	2.5
		1942	3.1	1962	2.4
1921	5.9	1943	2.5	1963	2.5
1922	5.8	1944	2.5	1964	2.6
1923	5.6	1945	2.9	1965	2.9
1924	5.8	Avg.	2.9	Avg.	2.6
1925	5.8				
Avg.	5.8	1946	3.5	1966	3.3
		1947	3.4		
1926	5.8	1948	3.3		
1927	5.6	1949	2.8		
1928	5.9	1950	2.8		
1929	5.5	Avg.	3.2		
1930	6.0				
Avg.	5.8				

*Data for 1910–1932 are for "Death-registration States" only; data for 1933–1966 are for the entire United States.

Source: Public Health Service, U.S. Department of Health, Education and Welfare (1910–1960); Federal Bureau of Investigation, U.S. Department of Justice (1961–1966).

I. 11. During this 57-year period in which the firearms homicide rate has shown this downward trend, the extent of firearms ownership in the United States has trended upward. These data are not at all consistent with a contention that firearms are a causative factor in homicides, but rather tend to refute such a view. Nor do the data suggest that the problem of the misuse of firearms in homicide is a new one which has suddenly appeared on the sociological horizon. Perhaps the increasingly efficient communications media of today are partly responsible for much of the public having this impression. While efforts must be made to solve the problem of the misuse of firearms in crime, the extent of the problem and its present status should be judged in terms of the entire period for which data are available. Only then can the problem be seen in its proper perspective and subjected to meaningful analysis.

Firearms in crime: 1966

I. 12. Firearms were misused in 3.4 percent of the 3,243,370 "serious" crimes that were committed in the United States in 1966. "Serious" crimes as defined by the FBI in the Uniform Crime Reports include murder and non-negligent manslaughter, forcible rape, robbery, aggravated assault, burglary, larceny ($50 and over), and auto theft. Murder and non-negligent manslaughter, aggravated assault and robbery are the three specific crime categories in which firearms are sometimes misused. Table 1 shows the relationship of firearms to other weapons used in the commission of serious crimes in 1966.

Table 2. Relationship of Firearms* to Other Weapons Used in the Commission of Serious Crimes, 1966

	Percent of weapons used	Total crimes committed	Crimes in which firearms were used
Homicide	—	10,920	—
Firearms	59.3	—	6,476
Knives or cutting instruments	22.3	—	—
Personal weapon (hands, feet, etc.)	9.4	—	—
Blunt objects	5.4	—	—
Miscellaneous	3.6	—	—
Aggravated assault	—	231,800	—
Knives or cutting instruments	33.6	—	—
Blunt objects	22.3	—	—
Personal weapon (hands, feet, etc.)	25.3	—	—
Firearms	18.8	—	43,578
Robbery	—	153,420	—
Armed with firearms	38.9	—	59,680
Other weapons	19.4	—	—
Strong arm (muggings)	41.7	—	—
Forcible rape	—	25,330	—
Burglary	—	1,370,300	—
Larceny ($50 and over)	—	894,600	—
Auto theft	—	557,000	—
Total	3.4%	3,243,370	109,734

*Firearms including the so-called gangster weapons as so classified under the National Firearms Act of 1934, zip guns, toy guns, alleged guns, pistols and revolvers, and rifles and shotguns.

Source: F.B.I. Uniform Crime Report—1966, and supplemental letter from the Director of the F.B.I.

I. 13. Unfortunately, data breaking down this 3.4 percent into (1) gangster weapons as classified under the National Firearms Act of 1934, (2) "zip guns," (3) toy guns, (4) alleged guns [where no weapon was actually seen but where one was suspected and was reported as being used], (5) pistols and revolvers, and (6) rifles and shotguns, were not available. Therefore, just what the role of each is in the total picture of the misuse of firearms in crime can only be estimated. It is possible to say that the percentage of serious crimes in which non-gangster type firearms are involved is less than the 3.4 percent figure, and that handguns, including zip guns, are the most frequently misused type of firearm.

I. 14. It is known, for example, that in 1966, pistols and revolvers, including zip guns, were involved in 72.7 percent of all *firearms* homicides, rifles in 11.4 percent, and shotguns in 15.9 percent. The latter two categories, of course, include an unknown number of gangster-type weapons, i.e. "sawed-off" rifles and shotguns and machine guns.

I. 15. According to Prosecuting Attorney William L. Cahalan's testimony before the Senate Subcommittee to Investigate Juvenile Delinquency in July of 1967, Detroit Police Department statistics indicate that 95 percent of all gun armed robberies in that city are with handguns.

I. 16. The Washington, D.C. Police Department reported that, in fiscal years 1964–1966, there were 10,348 robberies in the nation's capitol. Pistols and revolvers, including zip guns, were involved in 2,619, or 25.3 percent of the cases. Rifles and shotguns were used in 89, or less than one percent of the robberies. Of the total number of robberies which involved firearms, 96.7 percent were committed with pistols and revolvers and 3.3 percent with rifles and shotguns.

I. 17. FBI and New York City Police Department Statistics show that there were 23,539 robberies in the city of New York in 1966. Handguns were used in 23.4 percent of these robberies and rifles, shotguns and machine guns in 0.6 percent. Of the total number of robberies committed with all types of firearms, those committed with rifles, shotguns and machine guns constituted 2.3 percent.

I. 18. In all probability, these figures are similar to those encountered in other cities, as by and large, holdups are committed with concealable weapons. These data indicate that of all the serious crimes which occurred in the United States in 1966, less than one half of one percent (0.005) involved rifles and shotguns.

I. 19. In addition to the 3,243,370 serious crimes known to have been committed in 1966, there were nearly six million arrests for assaults, embezzlement and fraud, forgery and counterfeiting, arson, violation of narcotic drug laws, vandalism, vice and other crimes excluding traffic violations. With the number of such crimes amounting to more than four times the number of arrests made, the total number of crimes committed in the United States in 1966 was apparently no less than a staggering 31 million (excluding traffic offenses)![2] Thus, serious crimes

---

[2] The percent of offenses cleared by arrest in 1966 was 24.3 for serious crimes, and 21.1 for other crimes, excluding traffic offenses. A clearance of 21.1 percent for 27,871,800 crimes would account for 5,880,967 arrests as noted above. With 3,243,370 serious crimes having been committed, the grand total for all crimes, excluding traffic offenses, would be 31,115,170. This, of course, does not ac-

committed with firearms of all types constituted no more than 35/100 of one percent (0.0035) of all the crime in the United States in 1966. Such crimes committed with rifles and shotguns were probably no more than 5/100 of one percent (0.0005) of the total!

Conclusion

I. 20. In 1966, there were 3,243,370 serious crimes committed in the United States. Firearms of all types, including zip guns, gangster weapons, and alleged guns, were involved in 109,734, or 3.4% of these serious crimes. Rifles and shotguns were involved in less than one-half of one percent (0.005).

I. 21. The grand total of all crime, excluding traffic offenses, in the United States in 1966 was apparently in excess of 31 million. Serious crimes involving firearms constituted about 35/100 of one percent (0.0035) of this total. Such crimes involving rifles and shotguns accounted for approximately 5/100 of one percent (0.0005).

I. 22. What this means in practical terms is that if firearms were to be completely eliminated from society, (granted, an impossibility) and no criminal substituted any other type weapon for a firearm, the United States would still have 96.6% of its serious crime, and 99.6% of its total crime. If all rifles and shotguns were to be eliminated from society, and no criminal substituted any other type of weapon for them, the United States would still have at least 99.5% of its serious crime and at least 99.9% of all its crime. The fact that criminals do substitute other weapons for commercially-manufactured firearms is obvious, and has been well-documented. For example, the use of homemade zip guns exceeded the misuse of rifles and shotguns in murders, robberies, and assaults in New York state in 1966.

I. 23. Measuring the extent of the misuse of firearms in crime is a necessary prerequisite to evaluating the possible effect which firearms legislation might be expected to have on the crime rate. Data presented in this study show that crimes involving the misuse of firearms account for a minimal part of the total crime picture. Firearms legislation would be correspondingly limited in its effectiveness.

I. 24. Previous studies [including that recorded in III] have shown that the availability of firearms is not a causative, but only an incidental, factor in the 3.4% of total serious crimes in which firearms of all types are involved. Studies [such as that done in II] have also shown that there is no statistically significant difference in crime rates between those states having firearms licensing laws and those which do not.

I. 25. It is axiomatic that it is desirable to have laws prohibiting convicted felons, adjudged delinquents, mental incompetents, drug addicts, adjudged habitual drunkards and fugitives from justice from purchasing or possessing firearms. But many of those who espouse firearms legislation as a means of reducing crime

---

count for any unreported crime. Crime reports, incidentally, measure the number of crimes, not the number of criminals. The number of criminals is substantially less than the number of crimes committed [from Krug's footnotes — *Ed.*].

rates in the United States are doing the public a disservice by leading people to believe that such legislation will successfully solve the crime problem, or for that matter, even a significant part of it, when the facts dictate that it will not. Misleading the public in this way tends to reduce the public's justifiable concern over our alarming crime rate and delays positive action aimed at the real causes of crime. These, as many studies have shown, are socio-economic in nature.

I. 26. With 40 to 50 million Americans owning firearms for lawful purposes, the burden should be on those advocating restrictive firearms legislation to show that the legislation they propose is an effective means of preventing crime and reducing crime rates. Proof in the way of scientific evidence, duly treated by proper statistical methods, should be required. Emotional arguments based on personal opinion or political expediency should be rejected. Benefits, if any, to be gained from firearms legislation should be judged both in terms of the financial cost to the community and in terms of the subsequent loss of personal freedom and individual civil rights.

II. A Statistical Study of the Relationship Between Firearms Licensing Laws and Crime Rates

II. 1. Thirty-six of the fifty States regulate the acquisition and/or carrying of firearms—for the most part, "handguns"—by some form of licensing or prohibition, presumably with a view to prevent[ing] the misuse of firearms in crime. An evaluation of the effectiveness of these licensing laws necessarily entails a statistical analysis to determine the correlation, if any, between the licensing laws and crime rates in the various States.

II. 2. A rather comprehensive study on the possible relationship of firearms legislation (regulation) and crime rates was accomplished by the Wisconsin Legislative Reference Library for the Wisconsin State Legislature in 1960. The results of this study indicated that there is no demonstrable correlation between firearms regulations and crime rates. The study noted that other factors, such as geography, homogeneity of population, density of population, median school years completed, and per capita personal income, do appear to be significantly related to crime rates. The study also noted, interestingly, that firearms legislation (regulation) does seem to be related to a "great deal of paper work, particularly on the part of the retailer."

II. 3. In the present study, current data have been analyzed by statistical methods in order to ascertain if there is any statistically-significant difference in crime rates for the license and non-license States at the present time. Table 3 shows the level of licensing in the 36 license States.

II. 4. In connection with the licensing of firearms dealers and purchasers, it is to be noted that all firearms dealers, regardless of their State of residence, must keep complete records of all transactions as required by the Secretary of the Treasury under the provisions of the Federal Firearms Act of 1938. . . . These records

Table 3. Level of Licensing in the 36 License States

State	Manufacturer	Wholesaler	Retailer	Person possessing	Person purchasing	Person carrying
Alabama			X		X[1]	X
California			X		X[1]	X
Colorado						X
Connecticut			X		X[1]	X
Delaware			X			X
Florida					X[2]	X
Georgia		X	X		X[3]	X
Hawaii	X	X	X	X[4]	X	X
Idaho			X			X
Indiana			X		X[1]	X
Iowa			X			X
Louisiana		X	X		X[5]	X[6]
Maine						X
Massachusetts			X		X	X
Michigan			X		X	X
Mississippi				X[7]		X
Missouri					X	X
Montana						X
Nevada						X
New Hampshire			X			X
New Jersey			X		X	X
New York			X	X	X	X
North Carolina			X		X	X[6]
North Dakota			X[8]			X
Oregon			X		X[1]	X
Pennsylvania			X		X[1,9]	X
Rhode Island			X		X[1]	X
South Carolina[10]						X[11]
South Dakota			X		X	X
Tennessee			X		X[1]	X[6]
Texas		X	X			X[6]
Utah					X[12]	X
Virginia			X[8]		X[13]	X
Washington			X			X
West Virginia			X			X
Wyoming						X

[1] No permit to purchase, but administrative procedure of required waiting period between purchase and delivery of a handgun constitutes the equivalent of such a permit.
[2] Jacksonville and Miami.
[3] Columbus and Savannah.
[4] Hawaii requires the registration of all handguns with the police.
[5] New Orleans.
[6] No license to carry required, but carrying of a handgun concealed on the person is prohibited.
[7] Mississippi requires all firearms having a muzzle velocity of more than 2,000 feet per second to be registered with the county sheriff.
[8] Optional by cities or counties.
[9] Philadelphia bill 560-A requires a license to purchase any firearm (rifle, shotgun, or pistol).
[10] South Carolina law forbids any person, firm, or corporation to "manufacture, sell, offer for sale, lease, rent, barter, exchange or transport for sale into this State any pistol."
[11] Carrying prohibited.
[12] Salt Lake City.
[13] Virginia requires a permit to purchase a handgun in counties having a population density of more than 1,000 per square mile. The cities of Arlington, Norfolk and Richmond also require such a permit.

Source: Individual State and local statutes.

Table 4. Rates of Serious Crime, by State, 1965

License states	Murder & Non-negligent manslaughter	Robbery	Aggravated assault	Total "Serious crimes"
Alabama	11.4	28.7	149.1	1067.9
California	4.7	113.3	142.9	2643.5
Colorado	3.5	54.5	78.6	1544.3
Connecticut	1.6	19.3	43.5	1175.1
Delaware	5.1	54.9	28.1	1287.6
Florida	8.9	88.6	188.6	2010.9
Georgia	11.3	29.8	147.0	1199.7
Hawaii	3.2	18.7	46.3	1890.1
Idaho	2.0	10.1	53.6	927.3
Indiana	3.5	55.9	62.8	1217.9
Iowa	1.3	12.8	20.1	706.5
Louisiana	8.1	51.3	132.6	1184.0
Maine	2.1	4.0	30.4	680.0
Massachusetts	2.4	40.0	50.7	1507.3
Michigan	4.4	102.6	129.8	1734.8
Mississippi	8.9	14.4	139.9	690.8
Missouri	6.7	93.3	117.4	1602.5
Montana	1.7	15.9	47.5	1082.7
Nevada	8.4	97.5	95.2	2395.7
New Hampshire	2.7	6.9	11.7	610.5
New Jersey	3.2	55.4	86.3	1396.6
New York	4.6	61.3	117.5	1608.2
North Carolina	7.9	21.6	16.4	980.0
North Dakota	.9	4.6	23.6	501.7
Oregon	3.4	46.0	59.3	1486.9
Pennsylvania	3.5	51.4	72.0	968.8
Rhode Island	2.1	19.0	53.6	1417.9
South Carolina	9.6	21.4	134.9	1096.8
South Dakota	1.6	9.2	41.4	632.4
Tennessee	8.0	28.6	91.1	1082.9
Texas	7.5	42.0	137.2	1403.9
Utah	1.5	23.1	56.0	1394.3
Virginia	6.6	38.5	133.9	1158.6
Washington	2.2	30.3	60.4	1363.4
West Virginia	4.0	14.4	55.4	528.8
Wyoming	2.9	17.9	43.2	1001.6
Mean	4.8	38.8	86.1	1255.1
Non-License states				
Alaska	6.3	39.9	85.0	1709.9
Arizona	5.0	55.7	113.9	1934.5
Arkansas	5.9	23.7	95.9	739.9
Illinois	5.2	164.8	136.7	1613.1
Kansas	2.7	24.0	71.2	996.5
Kentucky	5.3	36.7	60.4	1051.6
Maryland	6.7	83.0	181.5	1718.2
Minnesota	1.4	40.3	39.5	1150.3
Nebraska	2.4	21.9	28.2	851.5
New Mexico	6.1	42.7	129.2	1514.4
Ohio	3.6	51.6	60.7	1038.7
Oklahoma	4.4	38.0	77.7	1150.0
Vermont	.5	4.5	10.8	579.4
Wisconsin	1.5	11.5	29.5	737.6
Mean	4.1	45.6	80.0	1199.0

must include the make, model, type, calibre or gauge, and serial number, if any, of each and every firearm (rifle, shotgun or pistol) received or sold, and the name and address of the person or business from whom the firearm was received, or to whom the firearm was sold, as the case may be.

II. 5. In addition to these records, which must be kept for ten years from the date of the transaction and made available to law-enforcement officers upon request, there are certain records which must be maintained under the firearms laws of several of the States. In most cases, however, the latter merely duplicate the former.

[Table 4 presents data for each State on the three crime categories in which the misuse of a firearm may be involved: murder and non-negligent manslaughter, robbery, and aggravated assault. In addition, Table 4 presents data for each State on "serious" crimes as defined by the F.B.I.: homicide, forcible rape, robbery, aggravated assault, burglary, larceny ($50 and over) and auto theft. In each case the crime rate figures represent offenses per 100,000 of population, and the source is the F.B.I.s Uniform Crime Report for 1965.[3]]

II. 6. The statistical hypothesis to be tested in this study is: *States with firearms licensing laws have lower crime rates than States not having such laws.* The mean crime rates for the various crime categories are listed in Table 8.

Table 5. Summation of Results: Statistical Analysis of Crime Rates for Licensing and Non-Licensing States, 1965

	Licensing states	Nonlicensing states	Difference	t-value	Is difference statistically significant?
Arithmetic means					
Homicide rate	4.8	4.1	0.7		
Robbery rate	38.8	45.6	−6.8	0.6618	
Aggravated assault rate	86.1	80.0	6.1		
Serious crime rate	1,255.1	1,199.0	56.1		

II. 7. It is immediately apparent from Table 8 that in the cases of murder, aggravated assault, and serious crime, the States with firearms licensing laws *do not* have lower crime rates than the non-licensing States. However, in order to test the hypothesis in terms of the robbery rates, it is necessary to apply a "t-test" (Student's *t*-Distribution) to determine if the difference in mean robbery rates is statistically significant or is merely due to random variation (chance).

II. 8. The formula for the appropriate "t-test" is

$$t = \frac{\overline{X} - \overline{Y}}{s\sqrt{\frac{1}{N_1} + \frac{1}{N_2}}}$$

[3] [Table 4 actually is a consolidation of four separate tables compiled by Krug — *Eds.*]

where $\bar{X}$ is the mean crime rate of the licensing group of states, $\bar{Y}$ is the mean crime rate of the non-licensing group, N_1 is the number of licensing states, N_2 is the number of non-licensing states, and s is the "pooled estimate of the standard deviation" (the assumption is here made that the two groups of states have unknown, albeit identical standard deviations).

II. 9.   The formula for s is

$$s = \sqrt{\frac{\sum X^2 - \frac{(\sum X)^2}{N_1} + \sum Y^2 - \frac{(\sum Y)^2}{N_2}}{N_1 + N_2 - 2}}$$

where X and Y are the variates of the licensing and non-licensing states, respectively, and the term $N_1 + N_2 - 2$ constitutes the number of degrees of freedom. Alder and Roessler define the latter as (1): "the maximum number of variates which can freely be assigned (i.e., calculated or assumed) before the rest of the variates are completely determined; that is, it is the total number of variates minus the number of independent relationships existing among them."

The number of degrees of freedom is ordinarily designated by v.

II. 10.   Substitution of the robbery data into these formulae yields a value for $/t/$ of 0.6618. For $v = 48$, $t_{.1} = 1.679$. Since $/t/ = 0.6618$, which is less than 1.679, we conclude that the probability of selecting from two populations with identical means and identical standard deviations two samples whose means differ by more than 6.8 (in absolute value) is considerably more than 10%, which indicates that the result is not significant. Therefore, the difference between mean robbery rates of the license states and the non-license states is not sufficient to warrant the conclusion that one is lower than the other.

II. 11.   These results indicate that the statistical hypothesis *States with firearms licensing laws have lower crime rates than states not having such laws* must be rejected.

II. 12.   [Krug then undertakes "to explain the results of the statistical analysis by reviewing the studies which have so far been made in this field." He reviews the following explanatory "theses":]

II. 13.   1. Crime is caused by socio-economic problems, not by firearms.

II. 14.   2. Firearms are involved in only 3% of all crimes in the United States. Therefore, firearms licensing laws, even if highly effective, would not be likely to cause any appreciable decrease in the overall crime rate.

II. 15.   3. Firearms laws have varying degrees of effectiveness. The degree of effectiveness determines the effect on the crime rate. Therefore, enactment of firearms laws is not automatically reflected in a reduction of crime rates.

II. 16.   4. The incidence of non-felony homicide is not related to the availability of firearms; when human inhibitions to kill are overcome, whatever weapon is readily available will be used. The easy availability of firearms does not make murder easy.

II. 17.   5. In the case of robbery and felony murder, experience of law-enforcement officials has shown that criminals are not deterred in their quest for firearms by firearms laws, and such individuals persist in carrying weapons regardless of any law which has so far been enacted.

II. 18. 6. Many firearms are stolen and available to the criminal through illicit channels. This limits the effectiveness of any law which regulates the acquisition of firearms through legitimate channels.

II. 19. 7. Criminals will substitute other weapons in the commission of crimes when firearms are not available. Legislation which prevents criminals from purchasing firearms is altogether irrelevant to the crime problem unless it can be shown that the end result was an actual reduction in crime, not just a reduction in the number of firearms possessed by the criminal element.

III. The Relationship Between Firearms Ownership and Crime Rates: A Statistical Analysis

Introduction

III. 1. It is estimated that there are some 200 million firearms in this nation, owned by 40 or 50 million Americans. There is at least one firearm in more than half the homes in the U.S., and last year more than 20 million Americans took part in various shooting sports.

III. 2. Claims that this widespread availability of firearms is a contributing cause to rapidly-rising crimes in the nation have been widely circulated by proponents of "anti-gun" legislation. Yet there is no reliable evidence to support such a contention. To date, not a single scientific study has shown a causal relationship between firearms and crime. This alleged relationship has even been written into proposed federal legislation. . . .

III. 3. This study shows that there is no statistical support for these claims. The statistics even demonstrate the opposite—that crime rates tend to be lower where the percentage of gun ownership is higher. These findings confirm other scientific studies which have concluded that firearms are not a cause of crime, but merely one of many incidental factors. [Specifically: Marvin E. Wolfgang, *Patterns in Criminal Homicide* (London: Oxford University Press, 1958), esp. pp. 79–83, and Romey P. Narloch, *Criminal Homicide in California* (Sacramento: California Department of Justice, Bureau of Criminal Statistics, 1967), esp. p. 55.]

Firearms ownership and crime rates

III. 3. If the availability of firearms were indeed a cause of crime, crime rates should rise and fall fairly consistently with rates of firearms ownership. States where a high proportion of the population possesses firearms should be expected to have higher crime rates than States where a lesser proportion of the population owned firearms. This proposition can be examined in the light of basic statistics available to all.

III. 4. Because the major use of firearms is for hunting, the number of individuals who purchase hunting licenses in each State is a reliable guide to the extent of firearms ownership in those same States. Table 6 shows the rate of hunting license holders per 100,000 of population and rates of serious crime [as previously defined by the F.B.I.], murder, aggravated assault, and robbery for each of

Table 6. Index of Firearms Ownership and Crime Rates for Each of the 50 States, 1966

State	Index of firearms ownership — Rate of hunting license holders[1]	Crime rates[2]			
		Serious crime	Murder	Aggravated assault	Robbery
Alabama	9,924	1,208.9	10.9	177.7	32.0
Alaska	15,719	1,866.6	12.9	82.0	36.0
Arizona	8,232	2,215.7	6.1	122.4	55.5
Arkansas	13,224	831.4	7.1	116.6	29.4
California	3,704	2,825.7	4.6	159.1	118.0
Colorado	14,152	1,718.4	4.0	93.8	53.8
Connecticut	2,200	1,306.1	2.0	45.8	20.9
Delaware	5,074	1,485.8	8.2	33.8	56.6
Florida	3,520	2,280.0	10.3	213.0	99.9
Georgia	7,344	1,309.0	11.3	142.6	34.9
Hawaii	961	2,077.1	2.9	53.9	21.6
Idaho	26,408	959.6	3.0	46.1	7.8
Illinois	4,282	1,729.7	6.9	156.4	184.9
Indiana	9,966	1,357.6	4.0	66.0	61.2
Iowa	10,284	814.0	1.6	25.0	12.8
Kansas	8,597	1,062.6	3.5	69.9	29.6
Kentucky	7,831	1,199.5	7.0	73.5	42.8
Louisiana	7,792	1,485.1	9.9	147.9	66.8
Maine	19,161	659.7	2.2	33.0	5.9
Maryland	4,927	2,062.3	7.0	164.9	123.7
Massachusetts	2,509	1,654.2	2.4	60.5	46.0
Michigan	11,070	2,174.0	4.7	136.3	156.0
Minnesota	11,009	1,317.4	2.2	44.4	49.4
Mississippi	12,005	587.1	9.7	119.6	13.3
Missouri	7,899	1,680.2	5.4	118.5	105.8
Montana	22,127	1,194.6	2.8	42.6	17.8
Nebraska	13,680	887.4	1.8	31.3	24.9
Nevada	14,183	2,360.2	10.6	98.5	96.9
New Hampshire	12,974	680.5	1.9	21.4	10.3
New Jersey	2,396	1,599.7	3.5	85.4	63.7
New Mexico	9,388	1,847.6	6.1	145.9	43.8
New York	3,854	2,399.6	4.8	155.2	142.5
North Carolina	8,347	1,086.9	8.7	248.2	22.8
North Dakota	11,774	560.5	1.8	23.2	6.2
Ohio	5,802	1,170.8	4.5	67.8	70.0

State	Index of firearms ownership— Rate of hunting license holders[1]	Crime rates[2]		
		Serious crime	Murder	Aggravated assault	Robbery
Oklahoma	9,591	1,282.9	5.5	81.2	40.6
Oregon	17,461	1,624.2	2.7	65.2	45.8
Pennsylvania	8,248	964.8	3.2	63.3	49.0
Rhode Island	1,576	1,732.3	1.4	62.7	25.4
South Carolina	7,747	1,210.4	11.6	172.0	28.7
South Dakota	20,498	775.6	1.5	62.9	10.0
Tennessee	9,442	1,275.6	7.8	105.2	34.4
Texas	5,587	1,607.3	9.1	149.2	54.7
Utah	19,528	1,652.3	2.0	65.2	36.5
Vermont	33,232	695.6	1.5	7.4	4.0
Virginia	8,100	1,249.2	6.5	132.9	42.9
Washington	10,550	1,579.2	2.5	72.4	36.7
West Virginia	12,969	591.1	4.2	61.5	19.1
Wisconsin	13,841	891.5	1.9	29.2	12.9
Wyoming	36,991	1,080.0	4.9	45.0	21.0

[1] Number of hunting license holders per 100,000 of population.
[2] Number of offenses per 100,000 of population.

Source: Bureau of Sport Fisheries and Wildlife, U.S. Department of the Interior (hunting license data); Federal Bureau of Investigation, U.S. Department of Justice (crime rates).

the fifty States in 1966. The first can be taken as a reasonable index of firearms ownership, and as such can be used in a statistical analysis[4] to determine the correlation, if any, between the extent of firearms ownership and crime rates. It does in fact constitute the best index available at the present time. In this way, it is possible to test the hypothesis "there is a causal relationship between the availability of firearms and crime rates."[5]

III. 5. Figure 2 is a graph of the index of firearms ownership and serious crime data.[6] The line of the graph represents the overall relationship of the various points on the graph, and was fit by the "method of least squares" [with the equation of the line taking the form $Ye = a + bX$, where a is the Y intercept and b is the slope of the line]. This "line of best fit," which slopes downward, shows

[4] Specifically, a regression analysis, which will (1) show if there is a relationship between the index of firearms ownership and crime rates and (2) enable any existing relationship to be expressed by means of an equation.
[5] Use of the rate of hunting license holders as an index of firearms ownership is consistent with the 1959 Gallup poll and the 1967 Harris poll on firearms, which proposed to measure the extent of firearms ownership on a regional basis. The Gallup and Harris polls cannot be used for the construction of a State firearms ownership index as the polls are unable to supply data on individual States because their samples are not large enough.
[6] Statistically, this graph is a scatter diagram, which is a graphical representation of a set of n paris of values of X and Y in a coordinate system. In this case, the X values are the index of firearms ownership and the Y values are the serious crime rates.

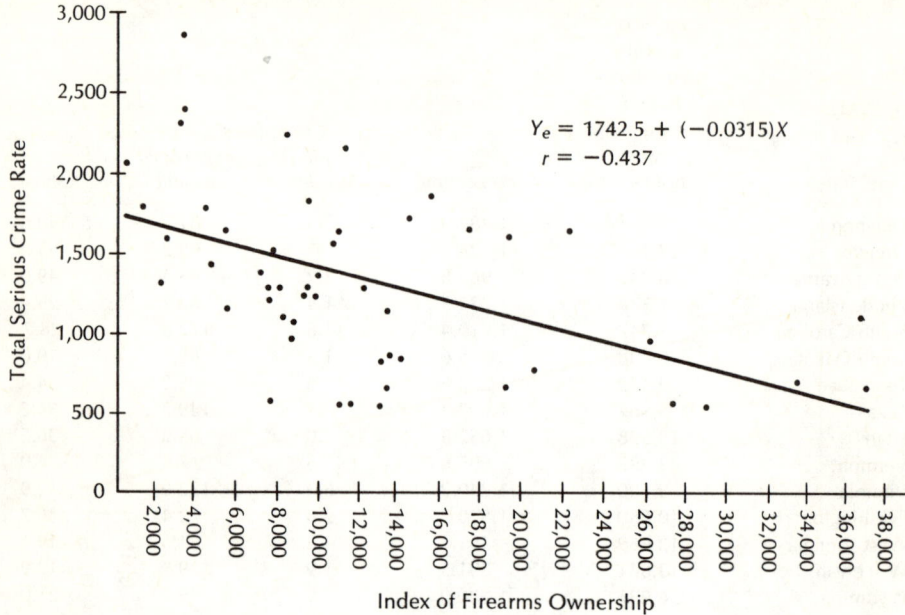

Figure 2. Correlation of Total Serious Crime Rates with Index of Firearms Ownership by State: 1966.

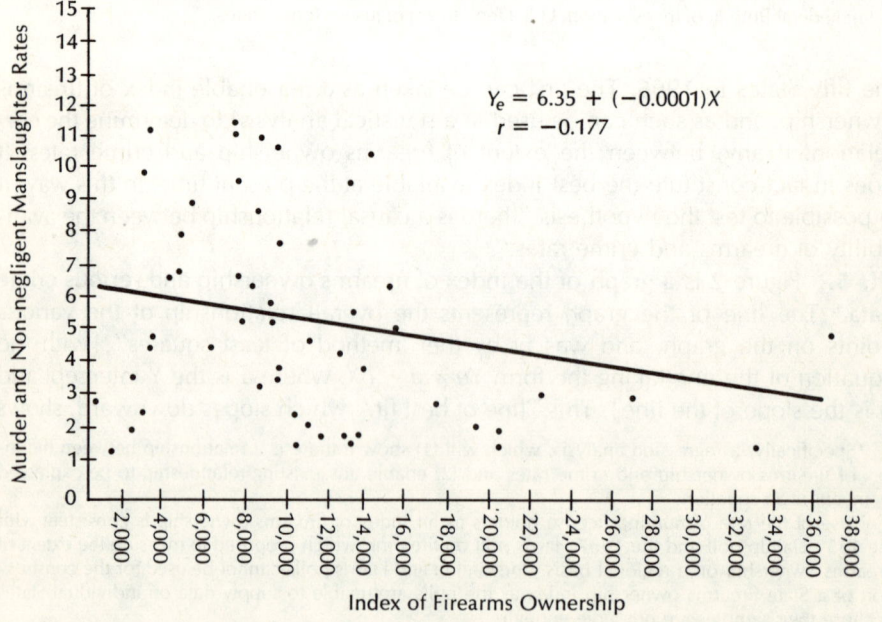

Figure 3. Correlation of Murder and Non-negligent Manslaughter Rates with Index of Firearms Ownership by State: 1966.

Appraising Policies

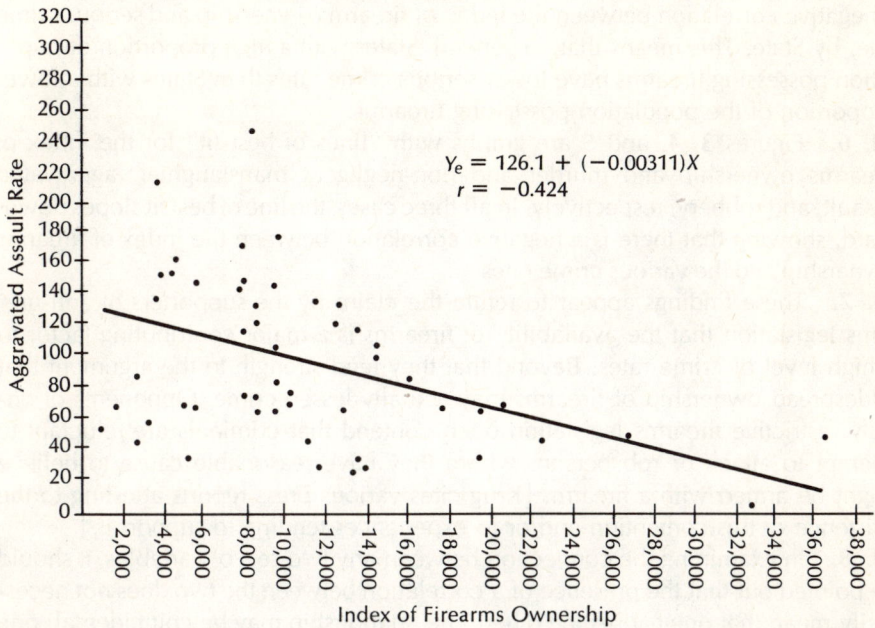

Figure 4. Correlation of Aggravated Assault Rates with Index of Firearms Ownerships by State: 1966.

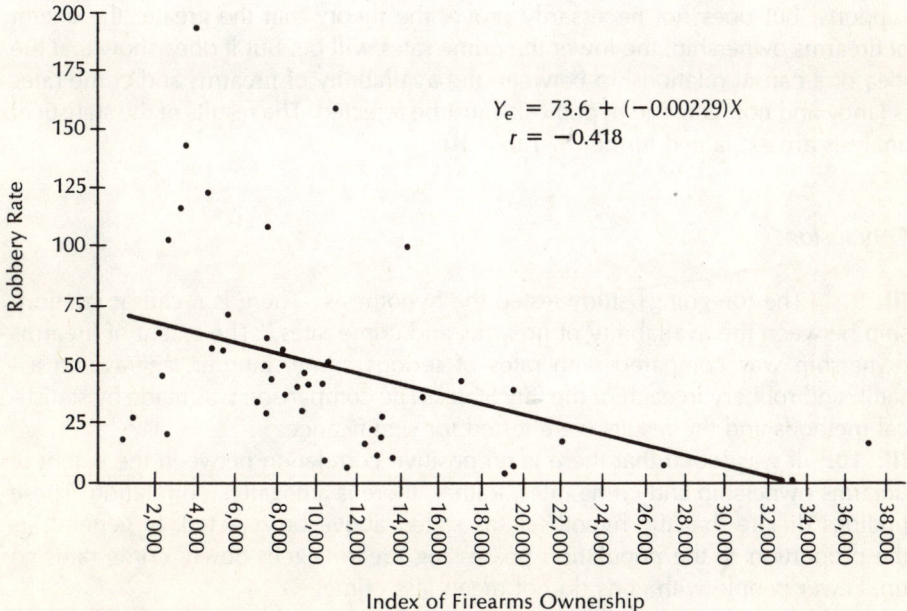

Figure 5. Correlation of Robbery Rates with Index of Firearms Ownership State: 1966.

a negative correlation between the index of firearms ownership and serious crime rate, by State. This means that, in general, States with a high proportion of population possessing firearms have lower serious crime rates than States with a lower proportion of the population possessing firearms.

III. 6. Figures 3, 4, and 5 are graphs with "lines of best fit" for the index of firearms ownership and murder and non-negligent manslaughter, aggravated assault, and robbery, respectively. In all three cases, the line of best fit slopes downward, showing that there is a negative correlation between the index of firearms ownership and the various crime rates.

III. 7. These findings appear to refute the claim by the supporters of anti-firearms legislation that the availability of firearms is a major contributing factor to a high level of crime rates. Beyond that they lend strength to the argument that widespread ownership of firearms may actually lessen crime. Opponents of unduly restrictive firearms legislation often contend that criminals are reluctant to attempt to attack or rob persons whom they have reasonable cause to believe might be armed with a firearm. [Krug cites various press reports attesting to the existence of this contention and/or to experiences tending to support it.]

III. 8. In examining the connection between any two sets of variables, it should be pointed out that the presence of a correlation between the two does not necessarily mean that one causes the other. The relationship may be coincidental; one variable may be a cause, but not the sole cause, of the other; the two variables may be interdependent; or the two variables may be affected by the same cause. Therefore, the negative correlation between firearms ownership and crime rates supports, but does not necessarily prove, the theory that the greater the extent of firearms ownership, the lower the crime rates will be. But it does show that the idea of a causal relationship between the availability of firearms and crime rates is fancy and not fact. The hypothesis must be rejected. The results of the statistical analysis are explained further in Table 10.

Conclusion

III. 9. [The foregoing] study tested the hypothesis "There is a causal relationship between the availability of firearms and crime rates." The extent of firearms ownership was compared with rates of serious crime, murder, aggravated assault, and robbery in each of the fifty States. The comparison was made by statistical methods and the results were tested for significance.

III. 10. It was found that there is no positive correlation between the extent of firearms ownership and crime rates. Rather, there is a negative correlation. These findings dictate that the hypothesis as stated above be rejected. In general, as the proportion of the population possessing firearms goes down, crime rates go up. Fewer people with guns do not mean less crime.

III. 11. The negative correlations between the index of firearms ownership and serious crime, aggravated assault and robbery were statistically significant. This

Table 10. Summary of Results: Statistical Analysis of the Correlation Between the Index of Firearms Ownership and Crime Rates, 1966

Correlation of index of firearms ownership with—	Equation of line of best fit[1]	Correlation coefficient[2]	t-value	Is negative correlation significant?[3]	Level of significance (percent)
Total serious crime	$Y_e = 1{,}742.5 - 0.0315X$	−0.437	3.36	Yes	1
Murder and non-negligent manslaughter	$Y_e = 6.35 - 0.0001X$	−.117	.76	No	5
Aggravated assault	$Y_e = 126.1 - 0.00311X$	−.424	3.26	Yes	1
Robbery	$Y_e = 73.6 - 0.00229X$	−.418	3.19	Yes	1

[1] The equations of the lines of best fit take the form $Y_e = a + bX$, where X is the index of firearms ownership, Y is the estimated value of crime rate obtained from the line of best fit for the corresponding value of X, a is the Y intercept, and b is the slope of the line of best fit.

[2] Correlation coefficients, r, indicate the extent of the linear relationship between each set of variables. Testing of the significance of the correlation coefficients was accomplished by applying a "t-test," where

$$t = \frac{r}{\sqrt{\frac{1-r^2}{n-2}}},$$

n being the size of the sample from which the data were obtained. The term "$n-2$" constitutes the number of degrees of freedom. The number of degrees of freedom is "the maximum number of variates which can freely be assigned (i.e. calculated or assumed) before the rest of the variates are completely determined: that is, it is the total number of variates minus the number of independent relationships existing among them.

For $n-2$, or 48 degrees of freedom, $t_{.01} = 2.686$, any value in excess of this being significant at the 1 percent level. This means that if a t-value in excess of 2.686 is calculated, there is no more than a 1-in-100 chance that the correlation is not significant. In such a case, it is a commonly accepted convention in statistics to consider the result highly significant.

[3] The correlation coefficients showing the extent of the linear relationship between the index of firearms ownership and (1) total serious crime, (2) aggravated assault, and (3) robbery are remarkably close in value. In all 3 cases, the negative correlation is highly significant, being so at the 1 percent level of significance.

Correlation of the index of firearms ownership with murder and non-negligent manslaughter is not significant at either the 1 percent or the 5 percent level. In the case where a result is significant at the 5 percent level, there is no more than 1 chance in 20 that the result is in error. Results are ordinarily not considered significant when the probability of error is in excess of 5 percent.

means that firearms ownership by the law-abiding public could be a factor in restricting the number of these criminal acts. However, such a cause and effect relationship is not proven by, but is only consistent with, the results of this study.
III. 12. These facts should be considered by anyone evaluating proposed firearms legislation.

Exercise 31. Minuteman Missiles: Scrap Them, Maintain Them, Strengthen Them?

The United States and the Soviet Union are capable of annihilating each other, and much of the rest of the world as well, in a matter of days. Their awesome capacity for mutual annihilation is embodied in guided missiles tipped with nuclear warheads, the individual destructive power of which exceeds that of millions of tons of dynamite.

Why have these weapons not been used in the past twenty-five years? One recurring answer, or one part of the answer, is that the nuclear weapons of the two countries counter one another. Neither nation can expect to survive, let alone to profit, from the consequences of seizing the initiative in nuclear warfare. Each nation possesses an abundance of "second strike capability." Each has nuclear weapons so numerous, so scattered, and so well protected as to be essentially immune to annihilation by the other side. If they were to launch an all-out nuclear attack on the United States, the Soviets could not escape a counterattack in kind. Their nuclear warheads could annihilate the people, the cities, the entire United States, but they could not pulverize United States' missiles with all their destructive power. And the United States operates under the same constraints. Accordingly the weapons systems of the two nations not only are engines of prodigious power to destroy but also are engines that deter such wholesale massacre. However, this Balance of Terror constantly undergoes alteration because of the changes in weapons technology and in levels of expenditure on strategic weapons.

The United States strategic nuclear arsenal has essentially three components: long-range bombers carrying nuclear guided missiles, Polaris submarines carrying long-range missiles armed with nuclear tips, and land-based long-range nuclear missiles. The latter missiles are called Minutemen. About 1000 Minutemen missiles are located at 100 sites in the continental United States, mostly in places away from major population centers. The missiles are planted in underground shafts. They are heavily shielded, so as to retain their capacity for launching even after an almost direct hit by an attacking missile on their housings.

Until recently, responsible experts voiced confidence that the Minuteman system was indeed capable of withstanding an all-out nuclear attack and thus of fulfilling its mission of deterring nuclear aggression. But in January 1969, President Richard M. Nixon suggested that conditions were undergoing an ominous change: The Soviets were developing a new order of nuclear missiles, a class of weaponry tending to make the Minuteman increasingly vulnerable to enemy attack. Nixon requested a $1.8 billion appropriation for deploying Safeguard, a system of antimissile missiles designed to neutralize the effects of the anticipated increase in Soviet capacity to pulverize Minuteman sites. He also requested an appropriation of $2 billion to improve Minuteman by adding Multiple Independently Targeted Reentry Vehicles (MIRVs) so that each missile could carry a cluster of nuclear weapons to an assortment of targets.

Nixon's request and Secretary of Defense Melvin Laird's accompanying testimony triggered a debate about the present usefulness of Minuteman. The debate took place within the context of public information to the effect that the United States surpasses the Soviet Union in supply of nuclear warheads, whereas the Soviet Union is ahead in supply of long-range missiles. Some congressmen contended that, far from being fortified, the Minuteman system should be scrapped. The bomber and Polaris fleets, they argued, are sufficient as nuclear deterrents, the Minuteman is obsolescent, and the Minuteman complex is a threat to rather than a source of American security.

Some of the recurring themes and arguments on this issue were recapitulated in a March 1, 1970 program of "The Advocates," a television series financed by the Corporation for Public Broadcasting and the Ford Foundation. The following transcript is a slightly edited and abbreviated version of that program.

Your assignment is (1) to complete a short-answer quiz and then (2) to compose a comprehensive evaluation of the presentations made by the participants in the debate. Details are given at the end of the debate.

Should Congress Scrap the Land-Based Missile Program?*

I. Opening Statements

I. 1. *Moderator Victor Palmieri:* . . . Tonight the issue is nuclear weapons. The practical choice, one which underlies the [Nixon] Administration's recent proposal for more anti-ballistic missiles, is this: "Should Congress scrap the land-based missile program?" We have two guest advocates, men who know and care about this question. The first is Dr. Jeremy J. Stone, foreign policy and arms control expert and currently a Fellow at the Council on Foreign Relations in New York. Dr. Stone says "Yes." [He proposes] that we scrap our land-based missiles, that Congress provide no money to maintain them, no money to improve them, and no money for anti-ballistic missiles to defend the Minuteman.

I. 2. *Advocate Jeremy Stone:* I'm going to argue that we should buy only what we need, keep our forces invulnerable, and throw away the obsolete. I'm going to show that the Minuteman missile is obsolete in a very important sense. It's lost public confidence, and there's no way to restore it. . . .

I. 3. *Palmieri:* Our other guest advocate tonight is Max Singer, an arms control expert and president of the Hudson Institute, a non-profit research center which studies foreign policy issues. Mr Singer says "No."

I. 4. *Advocate Max Singer:* I think the country needs to continue to buy insurance against the dangers of nuclear war, and I see nothing about the Soviet threat that has declined and that justifies us in throwing away a major part of our force unless we get something from them in return.

II. First Affirmative Witness: Direct Examination

II. 1. *Stone:* Minuteman missiles are obsolete. I want to explain to you what it means when a missile or a weapon is obsolete. It doesn't mean it won't work; a

---

*Reprinted by permission of WGBH Boston. This debate is a slightly edited and abbreviated version of a transcript of the 1 March 1970 program of "The Advocates," a television series produced by WGBH-TV and KCET-TV and financed by the Corporation for Public Broadcasting and the Ford Foundation. Responsibility for this adaptation of the transcript rests exclusively with the editors of this book.

lot of weapons we scrap will work. It doesn't mean necessarily the enemy can attack; a lot of weapons we have the enemy can attack. It means, especially and particularly, that we've lost confidence in it. It's a political matter. A political decision has to be made when a weapons system is obsolete. Minuteman missiles became obsolete when the Defense Department started to charge that they were vulnerable to enemy attack. The Defense Department called into question its own weapons system. It charged that the Soviet build-up would make these Minutemen vulnerable. This process of calling into question the weapons system has gone so far that there is no way to resurrect confidence in Minuteman, and this is what I'm going to show. My first witness will be Dr. Jerome B. Wiesner, the provost of Massachusetts Institute of Technology and . . . a man of great experience in this field who through the fifties and the sixties saw the development of the Minuteman program and the anti-ballistic missile program. I want to ask you first, Doctor Wiesner, whether or not you think it's worth the trouble, the effort, and the money to maintain land-based missiles in view of the scare which the Defense Department has already called up about the Soviet threat.

II. 2.   *Doctor Jerome B. Wiesner.* I don't think that it is.

II. 3.   *Stone:* [Do] you think confidence in Minuteman could be restored by putting an anti-ballistic missile system on top of these Minuteman missiles?

II. 4.   *Wiesner:* I don't think so.

II. 5.   *Stone:* Do you think an anti-ballistic missile system could be relied upon to work?

II. 6.   *Wiesner:* I doubt whether one could ever be made to work reliably.

II. 7.   *Stone:* If we threw the Minuteman missiles away, we'd have these 650 missiles on submarines—on Polaris submarines—floating under the ocean, invulnerable and so on. Would this be enough of a deterrent to deter the Russians from attacking?

II. 8.   *Wiesner:* I believe so, but we also have, of course, other components in our deterrent force: the bombers and the fighter bombers scattered all over the world.

II. 9.   *Stone:* And . . . if the present programs go forward, we'll not only have 650 warheads on these Polaris submarines, we'll have 5,000; and this is a process, already under way, which may begin in the next years and go over the next five years. . . . Five thousand warheads under the ocean would be enough alone to deter the Russians. I ask you, Doctor Wiesner, whether you think it's worthwhile to improve these land-based missiles with multiple warheads.

II. 10.   *Wiesner:* I don't believe it's worth spending any money to try to maintain these missiles in view of the fact that they have become vulnerable and in view of the fact that the Defense Department has made it very clear that they don't believe they're worth maintaining unless we build a very elaborate defensive system for them.

II. 11.   *Stone:* In other words, the Defense Department can require that we maintain these missiles, that we have an anti-ballistic missile system over it, and that we put multiple warheads on it; and the Minuteman is not necessarily a deterrent to the Russians in any case. Is that correct?

II. 12. *Wiesner:* That's correct.

II. 13. *Stone:* In fact the costs of such a program would be $10 billion to maintain, $10 billion to improve, and, to protect it, we don't really know how much, since it depends on how large the Soviet threat became. I want to ask you, Doctor Wiesner, since you're one of the very few people, one of only four people in this country, that know how the decision was made to build these Minutemen: Why did President Kennedy order a thousand Minutemen?

II. 14. *Wiesner:* Well, this was a partly political decision. The Eisenhower Administration had planned a diverse deterrent system that included some Minutemen—a number considerably smaller than a thousand. When the Kennedy Administration came into power, we were faced with an Air Force that was asking for 3,000 Minutemen. Some of us on the White House staff and in other parts of the government tried to stick closer to the Eisenhower levels, and the 950 number which was finally settled on was a compromise.

II. 15. *Stone:* In other words, in the first place, we didn't need so many Minuteman missiles. And isn't it true that at that time, we never thought you'd require 650 invulnerable missiles under the sea, much less 5,000, to deter the Russians?

II. 16. *Wiesner:* Well, I've always believed that a deterrent force could be a smaller force if it was secure—as I think a few dozen, or certainly a few hundred, warheads certain to be delivered on target is a sure deterrent.

II. 17. *Stone:* And if we kept our weapons secure, we wouldn't have a problem about these defense scares and this debate and all these problems. . . .

II. 18. *Wiesner:* The arms race will be exacerbated, I think, by taking any steps which perpetuate and build up the Minuteman for us.

II. 19. *Stone:* Do you think it's time that we looked into this question very carefully about deciding what it is we need? We should only buy what we need; how can we decide what is it exactly that we do need?

II. 20. *Wiesner:* Well, one has to start, of course, with an assumption about what you're trying to do, that is, what a deterrent is, and there's a big difference of opinion on this matter, of course. Then one has to also ask whether you're willing to play these very sophisticated numbers games, which some people enjoy doing and which trap us, I think very frequently, into running an arms race with ourselves, since we don't really know what the Russians are doing. Since there are very long lead times in most of the activities we're engaged in, we invent a weapon, then we invent the counterweapon, and we assume the Russians are doing both these things. And we do both of them, and then we talk about them, and sure enough, they do them. The MIRV, I think, is a very good example of this.

II. 21. *Palmieri:* Mister Wiesner, let me break in on you. Your answers to Doctor Stone's very pointed questions are so calm and complete I'm afraid you're going to end the program. Let's see if Mister Singer has some questions on cross-examination.

III. First Affirmative Witness: Cross-Examination

III. 1. *Singer:* At the time of the decision that President Kennedy made to set the size of the missile force, how many strategic long-range missiles did the Soviet Union have?

III. 2. *Wiesner:* I don't recall the exact number, but it was a relatively small number.

III. 3. *Singer:* And is your feeling about the subject changed by what the Soviets have done in the meantime?

III. 4. *Wiesner:* I am not particularly complacent about the Soviet SS–9 force, but I don't believe that a Minuteman force protected by an ABM system is really a very sensible way of responding to it. What we are doing with the Minuteman force—and what we will be doing if we add an ABM system to it—is just perpetuating a target system in the United States which makes the whole country a target; whereas if we depend on the sea-based deterrents, we've moved the targets away from our land.

III. 5. *Singer:* Doctor Wiesner, you're advocating that we do away with the 1,054 ICBMs?

III. 6. *Wiesner:* I would say that what I'm advocating is that we certainly not try to improve them; in fact, replace them with more sophisticated missiles and make an attempt to do something which I don't believe can be done, which is to protect them with an ABM system. Now, whether we do away with them tomorrow or whether we do away with them as fast as they become inoperable is a decision which somebody has to make after more study. [I'm suggesting] that they ultimately—sometime over the next several years—be phased out.

III. 7. *Singer:* Would they have any value as a deterrent, Doctor Wiesner, standing naked, that is, without any protection by the ABM?

III. 8. *Wiesner:* Well, they certainly have some now, and I think with passing time they will have less as the Soviet weapons develop greater and greater accuracy. I think they have been undercut, as Doctor Stone has said, by the Defense Department arguments—which I think have been vastly exaggerated—about their vulnerability, to the point where nobody is willing to give them any credibility today, although I think they still are an effective part of our deterrent system.

III. 9. *Singer:* Mister Wiesner, you've expressed a good deal of skepticism about the possibility of making systems work, particularly before they're installed. Now, I assume that the reason you feel that our Minutemen are so useless to us is that you feel that the Soviets will have a very great deal of confidence in the systems that they might use to destroy these Minutemen.

III. 10. *Wiesner:* No.

III. 11. *Singer:* Do you think such confidence would be justified?

III. 12. *Wiesner:* I don't believe they will; and what I believe is this: that the Minuteman by itself in its present form does represent some kind of deterrent. I don't believe that the Soviets could attack and wipe it out completely. On the other hand, I do believe that our attitude toward it is such that we can't stand still. We've created —

III. 13. *Singer:* —Are they designed to deter the United States or are they designed to influence the Soviet Union?

III. 14. *Wiesner:* Well, they are designed to provide a deterrent for the United States. On the other hand, I don't believe that it's a very sensible and economic thing to try to protect them with an anti-ballistic missile system.

III. 15. *Singer:* The question we have tonight is: Should we appropriate any money to maintain them? And if no money is [appropriated], they're not maintained, we can't improve them. So there's no money to maintain them; they have to go right this year, 1970. Would you be in favor of taking those thousand Minutemen out of their holes and throwing them away in 1970?

III. 16. *Wiesner:* As I said earlier, I'm not sure I'd throw them away in 1970, but I would certainly phase them out over the next several years.

III. 17. *Palmieri:* All right, Doctor Wiesner, thank you very much . . . . Mister Singer, Doctor Wiesner has made what seemed to be a calm and coherent argument, although in the end he seemed to stop short of "throwing them away," as you put it. However, he left little reason to keep them. Now, what's the case against the proposal to scrap them?

IV. First Negative Witness: Direct Examination

IV. 1. *Singer:* The problem of protecting our country against the dangers of nuclear war . . . is an old problem because we've been dealing with it successfully. Our success in protecting our country . . . for 25 years against the dangers of nuclear war has enabled us to turn attention to other, probably more urgent questions of domestic policy. All of us are concerned about being able to turn both our time and our money in national efforts to these problems because we feel safe with our nuclear forces. It is, therefore, tempting — in times when these other urgent questions come along — so say, "Let's forget about these long-run problems. We haven't heard so much about the Soviets' attacking us lately. Maybe we don't need any strategic forces against them." Let me urge you to try and take a long-run point of view toward this question of how much nuclear force is enough. Do we need to keep up our forces for the long run? I'd like to make it clear that there are two things that we all agree on. One, of course, is that we oughtn't spend any more money for defense than we need to. Secondly, nobody wants an arms race — an ever-accelerating, ever more dangerous spiral of defense expenditures. With those points accepted, then we have three questions which I'd like to discuss tonight. First of all: Are we spending more than we can afford? Secondly: What is the best way to get the Russians to limit their forces? And third: Is the Minuteman doing anything useful for us? On the Soviet side of the question, I'd like to call Professor William Griffith [of M.I.T.] who is an expert on Soviet foreign policy. Professor Griffith, has the Soviet Union changed in recent years in any way that makes them less dangerous to us? Are they any less willing to use force than they used to be? Have they stopped regarding us as their enemy?

IV. 2. *Professor William Griffith:* Well, they continually say that we are their enemy, and I'd be inclined to take them at their word. They're obviously not about to start a war tomorrow, but the main reason they aren't is that our forces are roughly equal to theirs, if not superior. In terms of their using force, it's a question you might perhaps pose more accurately in Prague than in Cambridge, or, for that matter—considering the fact that President Nasser [of Egypt] recently said that he's considering asking the Soviets to provide "volunteer pilots" to fight the Israeli Air Force—it's perhaps a question you might better ask in Israel than in Cambridge. The Soviets have, in general, been trying since [the Second World] war to expand their influence. They've made remarkable gains recently and I don't see much reason to assume that they're going to stop.

IV. 3. *Singer:* What have they been doing about their strategic forces in the last six or seven years?

IV. 4. *Griffith:* The important point, I think, is to see which way they've been going and which way we've been going. Since 1967 we've been pretty level. They've been coming up very strongly. At the present time, they're ahead of us in land-based missiles. And the fact that they are ahead of us in land-based missiles, when they could easily have given a signal to us that they were prepared to stop [at] being equal—which would have been at 1,054; but instead they've gone on to 1,350 or 1,400—is one of the many reasons why I personally think we cannot operate on the assumption that the Soviets will settle for equality with us, over all, in strategic missiles.

IV. 5. *Singer:* Can you mention some of the particular forces they've been building?

IV. 6. *Griffith:* Well, they've been building the SS–9, which is a 20-megaton missile with capability of destroying hardened missile sites. They've been building the SS–11. They, not we, started the ABM (anti-ballistic missiles). They, not we, have begun fractional orbiting bombardment systems. They, like we, are developing multiple warheads; and it's been said that their development is the sort that might make us think they're intended to knock out our missile sites.

IV. 7. *Singer:* Are their building programs showing any sign of coming to a stop?

IV. 8. *Griffith:* None that we can see. On the contrary, they're continuing, and they have been continuing, in land-based missiles and sea-based missiles and all these other systems.

IV. 9. *Singer:* Just to change the subject slightly . . . : How would they respond and interpret our action if we made a sudden cut in our forces, if we scrapped the major portion of our forces? What would they see that as meaning about our country and our policy?

IV. 10. *Griffith:* They would interpret it, I think, as a sign of weakness, as a failure of will. And in order to demonstrate why this is the case, let's look at the record of history. After World War II we demobilized most of our forces. President Roosevelt at the Yalta Conference told Stalin we would not keep any troops in

Europe more than two years after the war. Results: The Soviets expand over Eastern Europe and in 1948 start the Berlin Crisis. In the later 1940s we indicated to them that we would not defend South Korea. Result: The invasion of South Korea and another war. In 1961, when Kennedy and Khrushchev met in Vienna, Khrushchev obviously came to the conclusion that he could buffalo Kennedy. Result: The Cuban missile crisis. So, I can only conclude, with the French philosopher Voltaire—in terms of the proposal that we're debating this evening—that "those who do not learn from history are condemned to repeat it."

IV. 11. *Singer:* Since we are agreed that we have to try and get the Soviet Union to limit their forces, [then] the question is not whether to negotiate with the Soviet Union but how. Could you say something about how they bargain and how we best ought to behave to bargain with them successfully?

IV. 12. *Griffith:* They bargain hard; they bargain long; they bargain tough; but they bargain. And we should bargain with them. We've had considerable successes in bargaining with them, with the Non-Proliferation Treaty, with the Partial Test-Ban Treaty; and the initial contact at Helsinki on the SALT negotiations is promising. But the Soviets are very good at playing various games, and the one thing that one does not do, it seems to me, in starting to play a game, is what we have done so many times and have suffered for it: throw away some of your cards in the first round.

V. First Negative Witness: Cross-Examination

V. 1. *Stone:* Well, Professor Griffith, I think you've got the Russians right in some ways but wrong in others. First of all, [regarding] your quote of Voltaire: If the history we're talking about repeating has to do with the Korean war, the Vietnamese war, and other things like that, [then] that's not surprise attack. Do you think surprise attack—I mean nuclear surprise attack—is the Soviet style?
V. 2. *Griffith:* Only if they have overwhelming superiority.
V. 3. *Stone:* Do we kill people with missiles or with warheads?
V. 4. *Griffith:* Obviously, with warheads.
V. 5. *Stone:* Do we have now more targetable warheads than the Russians at this point?
V. 6. *Griffith:* Yes we do; but we had many more five years ago.
V. 7. *Stone:* Will we, five years from now—if present programs continue and the Soviet build-up continues at the present rapid rate—still have more separately targetable warheads than the Russians?
V. 8. *Griffith:* We don't know; and the reason we don't know is, we don't know what progress the Soviets will make with multiple warheads . . . and we don't know that [our planned progress] will be bigger or smaller than what the Soviets will do.
V. 9. *Stone:* The point I want to make here is that we are in no way standing still. . . . In fact, we are replacing Minuteman I by Minuteman II—an improve-

ment in effectiveness of a factor of eight. We'll move from Minuteman II to Minuteman III. We're improving our Minuteman missiles by a factor of three. [Figures which do not show this change are misleading; they do not accurately] reflect the strategic situation.

V. 10. *Griffith:* . . . You're talking about the future. You're proposing to play poker with the future and your first move in your poker game is to throw away a considerable number of your cards.

V. 11. *Stone:* No, I'm just telling you how to count the chips: count the warheads, not the missiles.

V. 12. *Interrogator:* Going back to the basic issue, Professor Griffith: If we do away with the land-based missile, will we still have a credible, effective deterrent [with Polaris] submarines [and] SAC bombers?

V. 13. *Griffith:* Less than before. And the result of it, in political terms, in Soviet conduct, will be the kind of conduct, including the kind of conducting in the strategic weapons negotiations, which we don't want. Once the Soviets are convinced that we're going to give away something for nothing—which I think Doctor Stone is proposing—this is not the way that makes them likely to come to a hard deal with us. On the contrary, they'll wait for a while and see if we won't give away more.

V. 14. *Palmieri:* . . . Don't you suppose that the more weapons that we have, the more the Russians feel they have to have?

V. 15. *Griffith:* That's undoubtedly true. And that's a very good reason why we should not try to build way ahead of the Russians. But the situation over the last few years—and we cannot predict the Russian future, we can only predict our future—but Doctor Stone does not know, and I do not know, how well the Russians will do. We can only talk about the immediate past. In that immediate past it is the Russians and not we who have been building up.

V. 16. *Interrogator:* Do you feel that the Russian extension of their missile numbers is a reaction to our deployment of ABM?

V. 17. *Griffith:* No; because it began long before we began to deploy ABM. Indeed, it was the Russians who first deployed ABM around Moscow and not we. [As for land-based missiles,] their build-up began, particularly in terms of lead time, long before we deployed ABM.

V. 18. *Stone:* Were we not talking about deploying an ABM every single one of those years and for the five years before? And isn't it true that if you wanted to prepare to penetrate ABM, you might have to start your land-based program in advance, just as we have started our MIRV program ten years before they got that missile defense system around Moscow?

V. 19. *Griffith:* [During each of those years] we decided not to [deploy an ABM], and still the Russians began to build up their missiles. The Russians began building up their missiles as a result of what they considered to be their defeat in the Cuban crisis and not because of talk in Washington about ABM.

V. 20. *Stone:* That's purely speculative.

VI. Second Negative Witness: Direct Examination

VI. 1. *Singer:* Professor Griffith has established the basic facts about the Soviet threat. They continue to be a dangerous country; lately they have been building their forces up very fast; it is possible to bargain with them, but you have to bargain close to the vest. Now I will introduce Professor Thomas Schelling [of Harvard], who will discuss our side of the strategic balance. Professor Schelling, what has been happening to our strategic forces in the last decade?

VI. 2. *Professor Thomas Schelling:* Basically, two things. The missile force has taken the shape that President Kennedy planned for back in the spring of 1961. . . . The bomber force has been drastically reduced: The B–47s are all gone; the B–52s have been about cut in half. Expenditures on these forces have actually declined by about a third and by somewhat more as a percentage of the defense budget. The strategic nuclear forces are a fairly small part of the total defense budget. It [they] excludes all the Army, most of the Air Force, most of the Navy. We're talking about possibly 10 per cent of the defense budget — 12 or 13 per cent if you add in the associated research and development. . . . There has been a very dramatic decline in explosive power carried by these missiles and bombers over the decade. Its nuclear megatonnage is greatly reduced. We've traded explosive power for more reliable weapons.

VI. 3. *Singer:* What role in our overall strategy did these missiles play — the Minuteman, the land-based missiles — which it's proposed today to throw away?

VI. 4. *Schelling:* Well, . . . I wouldn't want to own one. And, like Doctor Wiesner, I don't have confidence in the Minuteman. Unlike Doctor Stone, I also do not have confidence in the Polaris system or the B–52 bombers, but together the three inspire about as much confidence as nuclear weapons can inspire. I think the Russians take them seriously; they wouldn't be engaged in this kind of build-up, which a lot of people think is aimed at the Minuteman, unless they take it seriously. The land-based missiles are essentially one of the three systems we have. No one of them alone would inspire confidence. Think how we'd feel every time a nuclear submarine was lost at sea if all our deterrent forces were floating under radio silence on twenty or twenty-five boats. Think how we'd feel if our entire deterrent force depended on bombers in their second decade of age. Or think how we feel with the Minuteman force. It may not be able to survive an attack by those Soviet land-based missiles. None of them alone, I think, inspires confidence. I feel better about the Minuteman force knowing that we have the Polaris and the bombers there as a back-up. And I would stress this diversity. I would also stress that if we didn't have the Minuteman force, the Soviets might not have had to build up as big a land-based force themselves, and that amount of money put into submarine defense or bomber defenses might have further reduced our confidence if we had only one or two of the other systems. Like Doctor Wiesner, I suspect that Minuteman may become very susceptible to Soviet targeting in the years to come, and it remains to be seen whether it's worth the expense of replacing three-fifths of them, as is planned, with improved weapons, or [of] protecting them very expensively, as is also planned.

VI. 6.   *Singer:* What do you think might be the effect on the arms race if we, this year, scrapped our Minuteman force all of a sudden?

VI. 7.   *Schelling:* We wouldn't save much money, because the maintenance on the Minuteman is very, very small—the cheapest to maintain of all the strategic forces. My main concern would be how we would feel next year if we discovered an enormous missile gap of our own making: if we discovered that the bombers really wouldn't penetrate some new Soviet air defense; if we discovered that the Navy in arguing in favor of an advanced under-sea system lost our confidence in Polaris the way Secretary Laird apparently hurt Doctor Stone's confidence in Minuteman because he [Laird] wanted the Safeguard system. My worry is that the pressures to replace Minuteman, then gone, would be nearly irresistible. We've gotton used, over a decade—and so have the Russians—to the round number of one thousand Minutemen. There they sit. They're all bought and paid for. They're cheap to maintain. If we didn't have them and decided to start over because we needed them, I don't know what it would cost but my guess is [higher than Stone's] and the impact on the arms race would be a little bit like the old missile gap business of ten years ago, which I hoped we had overcome.

VII. Second Negative Witness: Cross-Examination

VII. 1.   *Stone:* Professor Schelling, in your book *Arms Control, Disarmament and National Security* you say that both sides, the United States and the Soviet Union, have a common interest in reducing the advantage of striking first simply because that advantage, even if common to both sides, increases the risk of war. In other words, a spiral of fear on both sides might encourage a war even when there was no deliberate attack. Most people interpret your writings to mean that if the land-based missile force from one side alone were eliminated, this spiral of fear could not take place, and the risks of the war that nobody wants would be substantially diminished, simply because there'd be no target for the other side to aim at—no advantage, therefore, in striking first. What do you think about that?

VII. 2.   *Schelling:* I think there would be a target for them to aim at and it wouldn't be in Montana and North Dakota. I also think, though—if we want to go back to what I wrote nine years ago—this is what President Nixon seems to have had in mind when he said that he would like to protect the Minuteman so that it was clearly intended to strike second, not first; and what I think he also had in mind when some people, who otherwise are very much interested in arms control, proposed that it would be far simpler to protect them by having them fire automatically upon receipt of electronic warning. President Nixon, I think, is suggesting that if we can make these weapons less vulnerable we will communicate to the Russians that [these weapons] are there to strike second, not first.

VII. 3.   *Stone:* Yes, but do you believe that just spending more money on the

Appraising Policies 131

missiles, leaving them with the same capacity to strike first, will make any difference in Soviet minds?

VII. 4. *Schelling:* I'd be happy to reduce their [the U.S. missiles'] capacity to strike first. I want to preserve their capacity to strike second. If we can't do it, if it proves infeasible, if the cost effectiveness of ballistic missile defenses looks bad, then I'd say: not scrap them, [but] leave them there at least to absorb into the Far West, the less populated part of the country. Don't scrap them, but don't expensively improve them.

VII. 5. *Stone:* Are you for protecting land-based missiles with an ABM; or are you just for keeping them, maintaining them without protecting them?

VII. 6. *Schelling:* My preference would have been to design a cheaper specialized active defense of hard points. I believe I would be [for protecting] but it would depend on whether effective, economical ways could be found.

VII. 7. *Stone:* You are for putting multiple warheads upon them as well, in the ongoing program?

VII. 8. *Schelling:* I haven't made up my mind on that one. I think I would, however—as the Administration plans to do—let the force be reduced in total number. The plan is only to improve and protect 600 of the thousand, partly because it's thought that the number of warheads will multiply and three-fifths of the present total is all that would be worth defending.

VII. 9. *Stone:* Let me draw your attention to this chart. It shows the cost of maintaining and improving Minuteman; but it also shows that the costs of protecting Minuteman are quite unlimited, because they depend on what the Soviet threat is. If we begin to protect Minuteman, by whatever kind of system—the ABM proposed by the Administration, or the one that Professor Schelling wants—we may have to continue adding radars and interceptors for the rest of our lives if the Soviet build-up continues. On the other hand, if we remove the land-based missiles, there aren't enough targets in the United States for the Russians to need any more missiles [to attack], and then we can say, "Ha ha, you're wasting your money on over-kill. There are no military targets to hit, just cities. You can destroy that anyway." The answer to the Soviet missile build-up is to remove the Minuteman from their target ranges.

VII. 10. *Schelling:* The same question might apply to keeping the Polaris system and the bomber system invulnerable in the future. Your figures are not my figures; but I'll go along with the fact that everything costs lots more than you expect, particularly with ten years of inflation involved here. If it proves a poor idea to protect Minuteman at these costs, we shouldn't. If it proves a poor idea to keep the bombers going at the cost required, we should rethink it. And the same with the boats at sea.

VII. 11. *Interrogator:* You say, then, that the land-based missiles are vulnerable? Are they more or less vulnerable than the sea-based missiles?

VII. 12. *Schelling:* Every weapon is vulnerable. In some respects [the land-based missiles are more vulnerable], in other respects less. If the entire deterrent force is on twenty-five floating platforms at sea or, alternatively, on a thousand dispersed hardened positions on the prairie, it's very hard to guess which is going to be more vulnerable to what. I have a hunch, for example, that the Polaris system is more vulnerable to a slow, undeclared war of attrition than the land-based missile. I'm quite sure that the land-based missile is more vulnerable to an unexpected, hastily-contrived, sudden attack out of the blue than the Polaris system. It is worth keeping in mind that the Polaris system is just as land-based as the Minuteman. [Polaris submarines] come ashore, and when they come ashore, there they are and they move out slowly, [although] not all at one time. Hardly over half, on the average, are likely to be at sea, especially if—favoring them as Doctor Stone does—we continually improve them and outfit them.

VIII. A Summation

VIII. 1. *Palmieri:* Let's hear Mister Singer's wrap-up on his case and then, Doctor Stone, we'll go to you.

VIII. 2. *Singer:* Professor Schelling and Professor Griffith have provided a basis for answering the question we started with. We can afford to continue to protect our country against the dangers of nuclear war. Even if the Russians spend a lot of money and build a big force, we are capable, and we can afford—and I think it is our responsibility—to continue the defense of our country. Secondly, there's not an ever-accelerating arms race. The Soviet's half of it has been accelerating lately; ours has not. Missiles are the way to count if you're interested in target points. They are [the way to count] if you're interested, in many ways, in money. They are the traditional way of counting, and they are entirely relevant. The best way to get the Russians to limit their forces is to bargain tough with them, not to give them anything for free.

VIII. 3. *Palmieri:* Well, Doctor Stone, Mister Singer says we can't afford to give up land-based missiles. What's your answer?

IX. Second Affirmative Witness: Direct Examination

IX. 1. *Stone:* I'm now going to call my political witness, Congressman Donald Fraser of Minnesota. Congressman Fraser, isn't it true under the Constitution that it's the job of people like yourself and the Congress and the Senate to decide on the gross outline features of our strategic force? In other words, ultimately a *political* decision has to be made about whether these missiles are worth maintaining?

IX. 2. *Congressman Donald Fraser:* Right.

IX. 3. *Stone:* Do you have political confidence—do you think the country has political confidence—in the Minuteman missile force?

IX. 4. *Fraser:* I think the problem of maintaining confidence in it is that the confidence in the Minuteman has been undermined by the Department of Defense

Appraising Policies 133

itself. And I've been looking at Secretary [of Defense] Laird's last posture statement, in which he suggests that if the Soviets keep on doing what they're doing now—I think there's every expectation that they'll keep on doing what they're doing now—[then] in fact there is no adequate way to protect the Minuteman missiles.

IX. 5. *Stone:* I think I want to emphasize what Congressman Fraser said, because most people haven't read this very posture statement. Last year the Defense Department said that Safeguard would be protection against the possibility that we didn't reach agreement with the Russians. This year the Defense Department's statement says Safeguard will only defend the Minuteman if the Russians stop immediately building more SS–9s and building MIRV. In other words, what was supposed to be protection against the possibility of failure to reach agreement with the Russians is now only an answer *if* we reach agreement with the Russians. What will they say next year? Do you have confidence, Congressman Fraser, in the ability of an anti-ballistic missile system to reestablish confidence in Minuteman?

IX. 6. *Fraser:* No, I do not.

IX. 7. *Stone:* How would you characterize this problem of putting land-based missiles underneath a missile defense? What sort of confidence can that bring?

IX. 8. *Fraser:* Well, the problem is that in the Senate of the United States, on a fifty to fifty vote, there was in effect a declaration of lack of confidence; and I think what's crystal clear is that the moment that we began to put an ABM in place the military itself would then find reasons to indicate its vulnerability, because they would then want to go to new technology, new systems, new hardware; and this has been the pattern of the past, so that they would then join in undermining the confidence.

IX. 9. *Stone:* In other words, putting a land-based missile under missiles is not like putting them under land or under water. People may change their mind about their calculations. But let me ask you whether money is in tight supply in Washington and whether or not we should save as much as we can, buy only what we need, and keep that invulnerable.

IX. 10. *Fraser:* I wish we would follow that policy. We're very hard up for money to meet some of our domestic needs.

IX. 11. *Stone:* Isn't it important to avoid having debates in the House and the Senate, which take so much time and energy that should be devoted to starting new domestic programs and so on? Isn't it better to have forces we don't have to debate about every year?

IX. 12. *Fraser:* If we could have forces that were invulnerable and that's all we had, and we didn't have peripheral or marginal forces that were subject to attack by the Soviets—I think our Minuteman missiles are—then I think we could get about our other business.

IX. 13. *Stone:* So you are not for improving or protecting Minuteman?

IX. 14. *Fraser:* I am not.

IX. 15. *Stone:* What is your feeling about maintaining Minuteman?

IX. 16. *Fraser:* Well, if we abandon Minuteman missiles—and I don't think they're worth maintaining—then we probably need to look toward building up our seagoing capacity: the Polaris submarine or other kinds of water-based, underwater-based missiles. And I would expect that we should move ahead with that.

IX. 17. *Stone:* So you believe that we should move ahead with the development with a new sea-based force and buy only if we need it. [And] you've argued that we should scrap the land-based missile program.

IX. 18. *Fraser:* Right.

IX. 19. *Stone:* You haven't decided the question of exactly the rate at which we phase [the Minuteman system] out, or whether we do it tomorrow. Just as Doctor Wiesner said, this is a matter for study. But you're for scrapping the program.

IX. 20. *Fraser:* Well, one of the suggestions that have been made is that we might take our Minuteman missiles, put them out to sea where they are not targets that invite Soviet attacks on the mainland of the United States. If they are going to attack them, at least [the missiles] will be out on the ocean, which is a little bit better than having them in the middle of our population centers.

IX. 21. *Stone:* In other words, once we decide we're going to scrap the program, then there's no question of improving them; then there's no question of protecting them; then there's no question of debating about them; then the rest is left to analysis, the minor costs of maintaining them until they're phased out. We decide on what we need to supplement them—if we need anything to supplement them. But basically we all agree—you and Doctor Wiesner—we should scrap the land-based missile program in a reasonable, sensible way.

IX. 22. *Fraser:* Right.

X. Second Affirmative Witness: Cross-Examination

X. 1. *Singer:* I think we need to clarify the question we have. The question is: Are we in favor of scrapping the Minuteman force? *not* Are we in favor of replacing it as new and better weapons come along, as the proper mix of equipment changes over time? It has changed from the beginning. All of our forces involved were bombers, first. We built the Atlas and Titan and decided those weren't the best. We went to Minuteman I, II, III. Polaris gave way to Poseidon—all of these changes. Now, you agree that that's the kind of process that ought to continue to go on and not that a piece of the force should suddenly be dumped—which would have to be, if there was no money for them.

X. 2. *Fraser:* Your question tends to obscure the problem itself. We're talking about land-based, fixed-site missiles. I think those are obsolete. I wouldn't want to go ahead with advances in that area, and I think that's what people who want ABMs, who want a MIRV, who go from Minuteman to Minuteman III, are talking about.

X. 3. *Singer:* But you want to scrap them before a replacement is available?

Appraising Policies

X. 4. *Fraser:* Our present program of MIRVing our submarines is more than adequate. I'm concerned about the fact that we're MIRVing even those. The Polaris missile, which is fired from submarines underneath the oceans today, is quite an adequate deterrent and will continue to be so for a long time to come, according to the Department of Defense and according to everybody else.
X. 5. *Singer:* In other words, you're saying that you would *not* scrap the land-based missiles if we did not have another alternative which is more effective.
X. 6. *Fraser:* That's right. I think we have it already in the Polaris submarines.
X. 7. *Singer:* Would you be willing to spend additional funds then for the Polaris?
X. 8. *Fraser:* For the Polaris; and I think it would be prudent to investigate other forms to try to get a longer-range missile that could be put out at sea.
X. 9. *Singer:* Do you have any idea what this would cost?
X. 10. *Fraser:* Well, we have some estimates. It depends a little bit of course on how rapidly we have to deploy them, but for the ULMS—the Undersea Long-Range Missile System—there has been a request, I think—it was a request for fiscal 1970—for twenty million. I think ten was granted. [This was] for development costs. It's estimated that if we went to a full-scale ULMS as a replacement for the Polaris and everthing else, it might ultimately reach twenty-five billion, but I think that's quite a ways ahead. I think the question is: How well would it prove itself to be, and how rapidly would we have to deploy it, measured against the Soviet capabilities?
X. 12. *Singer:* The questions of the validity and vulnerability of various systems; how fast the Soviets will be able to find something that may be able to attack submarines, and thus get sixteen missiles and 160 or more warheads at the same time; whether or not they'll be able to penetrate a system designed to defend Minuteman; and how many would penetrate what countries—these are all very technical questions, aren't they?
X. 13. *Fraser:* Yes, but I think essentially irrelevant. The principal question is: Can we impose on the Soviets sufficient destruction so as to deter them from attacking us? We can, today, and I don't see any reason why we can't five and ten years from now, even with the forces that we have.
X. 14. *Singer:* We can, today, even without the land-based missiles?
X. 15. *Fraser:* That's right.
X. 16. *Singer:* Now, you're going to be talking about arms control. Do you feel that your bargaining position will be strengthened if, before you go over there, we throw away a portion of our forces?
X. 17. *Fraser:* Let me say I don't have a lot of confidence in bargaining with the Soviet Union. I think that what the United States has got to do is to decide where its self-interest lies, what it needs to protect itself, buy what it needs, throw away what it doesn't need, and make sure that we're always safe and secure. And it's on that basis that I think we can get rid of the land-based missiles.
X. 18. *Singer:* I gather you're saying that the domestic budget has been so stinted that we cannot afford our offensive forces. I'd like to call your attention

to this graph. This [smallish-sized portion] is the amount of offensive forces budgeted for this year and out of this the Minuteman is paid for. This includes more than the Minuteman. In the same period of time, this is what the governments—federal, state, and local—are spending for domestic budget. These are all our domestic efforts, versus all our offensive forces including bombers, Polaris, Minuteman, and all their protection and so forth. Now, if you think we cannot afford this much money, how much money do you think we can afford for the protection of— —

X. 19. *Fraser:* You're asking the right question. But the fact is that on one of the billions out of the total layout of some three hundred billion, the President vetoed a major health–education–welfare bill. He thought that one billion added on for education and welfare was too much—that this did too much to the internal economy of the United States. So you can talk with these figures, but I think you've got to recognize how these come out to the crunch.

X. 20. *Singer:* How much of the rest of it goes for defense of the offensive forces? Is that included?

X. 21. *Fraser:* Yes. The defense of the offensive forces . . . in this period it's a very small amount of money, under a billion dollars.

XI. The Summations

XI. 1. *Stone:* Our Minuteman missiles became obsolete for two reasons. Soviets continue their force build-up, producing a force on a rough, comparable level to ours. In some ways we're ahead, and in some ways they're ahead. The Defense Department interpreted that build-up as so threatening that it said that our own Minuteman missiles needed an anti-ballistic missile system to protect it. I think their computations were too conservative. I don't think the Soviet build-up is that threatening; but I think that what the Defense Department has called in question, no man can put back together again. They have produced enough concern about this missile force so that half the country thinks it's in question. Our deterrents have to be above question. A foreign aid bill can be in question, but a deterrent should be above question. This deterrent is not above question, and a missile defense cannot be used to restore confidence in Minuteman, because missile defenses are the most controversial weapons systems we know, and they've been argued about for ten years and no one has any confidence that they can be sure to work the first time. They might work but we can't be sure. Our deterrent needs better protection, not because the Russians are so likely to attack us [but] because if it doesn't have high confidence protection, this country itself will worry and fret, buy more than it needs [and] have these kinds of defense scares that take so much time and money. I want to remind you what President Roosevelt said in 1932. He said: "We have only to fear, fear itself." By that he didn't mean that we didn't have problems. He meant we did have problems but we could control those problems if we could control the fear. Throwing away obsolete weapons is what we have to do in order to control the fear. And if we can do that, we'll be able to buy what we need, keep it invulnerable, and throw away the obsolete.

XI. 2. *Singer:* I don't think that this attack on the Minuteman forces, this proposal to suddenly scrap a major portion of our forces, is the way to avoid discussion of strategic issues. I don't think it's the way to avoid fear. I think it is characteristic of the arms race. It's characteristic of the problem of nuclear war that all our systems are going to have doubts about them, all our methods to protect them are going to have doubts. We have to learn how to live with those doubts in the long run. We have to, I agree, not have any systems that we don't need, not spend more money than we can afford, not indulge in an ever-increasing arms race. But if current Minuteman systems decrease the chance that the Soviets will get confused—the purpose of a deterrent force is to put doubt in their mind, not put doubt in our mind. Minuteman force does that. If by any chance we found ourselves in a war, we'd rather have more missiles than less missiles, and we do not want to decrease the chances that we will be without what we need in that situation. Are we spending too much? No; not by the measure of what we spent in the past, not by the measure of what the Soviets are spending. Does keeping Minuteman mean an accelerating arms race? Are we on an ever-upward spiral? No. We have phased out two-thirds of our bomber force. Soviets are increasing rapidly now; we are not. Finally, the only way to get the Soviets to stop is by tough bargaining with them, not by throwing away our force and encouraging them to think that if they wait, we'll throw away the rest of it.

Test I

1. List three arguments advanced by the Affirmative side in the foregoing debate—that is, by the proponents of scrapping the Minuteman missile system—and cite the places in the text where these arguments were voiced. Do not discuss the validity, cogency, or conclusiveness of these arguments, but rather identify, in a few words, the arguments themselves. (In the context of a policy dispute an "argument" is an avowed "reason" for adopting a course of action. The "reason" consists of a claim about cause and effect, as well as, implicitly, a claim about desirable effects).

2. Similarly, list three arguments advanced by the Negative side, and cite their location in the text of the debate.

3. Name one Affirmative or Negative argument that you deem weak "on its face" (not persuasive even if its factual claim is true[1]). Briefly state why this argument is weak "on its face."

---

[1] Suppose an advocate says the equivalent of the following: "we should adopt policy *p* because it will foster value *v*." This argument would be deemed weak "on its face" if *v* is regarded as being devoid of positive value. In that case, the factual claim that *p* fosters *v* would be deemed unworthy of being verified.

Test II

Compose a comprehensive essay in which you make a judgment as to which side presented the most persuasive case, and then defend that judgment.

In stating and defending your assessment, you should pass in review each important line of argument emanating from each side and the evidence supplied on behalf of each line of argument. Moreover, in preparing your critique you may find the following suggestions helpful:

a. A well-organized critique is analytical and substantive in character, dealing systematically with lines of argument advanced and disputed. A poorly organized critique is merely chronological, giving a blow by blow account of who said what.

b. A thorough critique itemizes the principal arguments advanced by each side (with suitable references to passages in the text) and takes note of what contentions were and were not substantiated, as well as what contentions were and were not challenged.

c. A careful, penetrating critique dissects arguments. For example, it calls attention to ambiguities (giving different meanings to a key term at different points) and to alternative measurements (such as how to gauge the costs of a given policy or program).

d. A constructive critique shows sensitivity to conspicuous *omissions*. For example, it suggests propositions that deserved major rather than passing attention, or propositions and lines of argument that were not canvassed although they deserved to be canvassed.

Index

Academic achievement, and radicalism, 34–36
Activists, student. *See* Radicalism
Alsop, Joseph, 5
American Institute of Public Opinion, 3
Anarchism, 57
Anarcho-syndicalist movement, 61
"Athleticism," and neurosis, 16–27
Attitudes, 2
Augur (auspex), 1

Bay, Christian, 28, 42–43
Birnbaum, Ed, 80
Bureau of Applied Social Research, 55
Bureaucracy, 45, 63, 64, 65, 75
Busing, opinion on, 8

Camus, Albert, theory on rebellion, 39–40
Canvassing, 8
Capitalist industrialization, 48, 62. *See also* Industrialization
Causation: multi-variate, 64–65; social, 27
Cause and effect, 13–14, 64
Cheating, on examinations, 5–6
Claghorn, Homer, 7–8
Class struggle, 56
Communism, 31, 50, 57, 61
Conditions: objective, 2, 3–7; subjective, 2, 7–11
Conservatism, 31–33, 36, 58
Craft-union movement, 61

Davis, Kingsley, 66
Death rate: age-specific, 4; and environmental conditions, 3
Defense capabilities, of aircraft, 5
Democracy, 43–65; and affluence, 46–47, 59; conditions affections, 43; and education, 50, 53–54, 59; and industrialization, 50, 53; and Protestantism, 62–63; and urbanization, 50, 53
Deprivation neurosis, 18, 25
Despotism, 46
Dictatorship, 49, 50–53
Differential association, 14–15
Distribution: of scores, 6; and social stratification, 66–68
Doctor Little, 16–18
Dogmatism scale, 31

Economic determinism, 61
Economic development: and class struggle, 56–60; and democracy, 46–65; in Europe and the Americas, 50–56; politics of, 60–63
Education: and democracy, 50, 53–55; indices of, 52
Elections, 3, 9
Electoral participation, 4
Electorate, 3, 9
Engels, Friedrich, 61
Equality, 65–66
Equity: in rent control, 83; and wage–price, 79
Errors, sources of, 1

Escalation, 8
Evidence: crude, 1; factual, 2; insufficient, 1, 3; statistical, 3

Family size, and delinquency, 15–16
Firearms: legislation, 108–113; misuse of, 101–108; ownership, 113–119
Fitzhugh, George, 84
Free society, 87–89, 94
Free Speech Movement, 34–36, 39, 42
Free trade, 85–87, 93, 95–96
French Revolution, 65

Gallop, George, 3, 9–10
Gallop poll, 9–10
Gore, Albert, 9–11
Government, role in society, 71–73
Grading, of student performance, 79, 80–82
Gun control, 99–119. See also Firearms

Homework, student opinion on, 7

Industrialization: and capitalism, 48, 62; and democracy, 50, 54, 60–62; indices of, 51, 53
Inference: causal, 14; factual, 1, 2, 5; false, 13; premature, 3
Institutional change, 56
Institutions, 48, 56
International Urban Research, 53
Iron law of oligarchy, 43–47

Juvenile delinquency, 14–16, 27

Kennedy, John F., 10, 16, 79, 99
Knowledge: spread of, 5; technical, 73–74
Krug, Alan, 101

Labor movement, 61–62
Law enforcement, 4
Leftist politics, 31, 33, 57, 61. See also Radicalism; Socialism
Lerner, Daniel, 55–56
Libertarianism, 33–34, 42
Liberty, 83–84, 95–98
Lipset, Seymour, Martin, 47
Literacy, 54–56

Marx, Karl, 58–59
Marxism, 61, 62
"Mass society," 60
Michels, Robert, 43, 44–46
Minuteman missiles, 119–138

Modernistic problems, 2
Modernization, 56
Monitoring, systematic, 2
Moore, Wilbur, 66

Nepotism, 60
Neurosis: incidence of, 25; and physical fitness, 15–27; and social influences, 26–27
Neurotic syndrome, 27
Nuclear weapons, 119–120; arguments against, 125–132; arguments in defense of, 121–125, 132–136

Oligarchy, 43–47, 50
Opinion: on busing, 8; on escalation, 8; on homework loads, 7; quality of responses, 9; on tax reform, 7
Opinionation scale, 31
Opinion survey, 2–3, 7, 8, 54. See also Gallop poll; Roper poll

Parry, Geraint, 44
Peronism, 50
Physical fitness, 16–17. See also "Athleticism"
Political analysis, 77
Political attitudes, 30–33
Political forms, 43–65. See also Democracy
Political participation, 4
Political system, 45, 47–48; and economic development, 50
Polling, 9–10
Pollsters, 3
Prejudice, 37
Premise, factual, 1, 2, 4–5
Productivity, 79
Progress: medical, 4–5; social, 5
Proletarian elite, 45–46
Public opinion, 2–3, 9

Quality control, 6–7

Race, and delinquency, 14
Radicalism: and intelligence, 28–29, 42; and personality, 30–33; political, 57–58; psychological theories of, 36–41; student, 27–43; studies of, 28–30, 33–36
Rebellion, 39
Redistribution, of wealth, 58, 60
Reliability, testing for, 8
Religion, 70–71, 72
Representativeness, 3, 8
Rightist politics, 31, 36. See also Conservatism

Roper, Elmo, 9
Roper, poll, 9
Russian Revolution, 62

Sample: selection of, 8; size of, 3
Samuelson, Paul, 79
Secular reformist gradualism, 56
Slavery, 83–84, 87, 88, 90–91, 92–94, 95–96
Social acceptance, 38
Social causation, 14–15, 27
Social disorganization, 55
Social forms, 65–76. *See also* Equality
Social scientists: assumptions on political forms, 46–47; and policy-making, 77–78; tools of, 1
Social stability, 56
Social stratification, 59, 63; functions of, 70–74; necessity of, 67–68; principles of, 66–67; types of, 76; variations in, 68–69, 74–76
Social supports. *See* institutions
Social system, 48, 63–64, 65
Socialism, 57, 62, 87–91

Statistical correlation, 14
System, competitive and non-competitive, 67. *See also* Social system

Tax reform, 7
Toleration, 29–30, 42
Trends, 2
Trotsky, Leon, 62
Tyranny, 50

Unions, 61
Urbanization: degree of, 53; and democracy, 50, 54, 55, 56, 64

Validity, tests of, 14
Value system, 47–48

Wealth, 50, 54, 58, 60; distribution of, 58–59; indices of, 50–51, 53; role in society, 72–73. *See also* Economic development
Weber, Max, 45, 58, 62, 63